Cambridge Elements ≡

Elements in Earth System Governance
edited by
Frank Biermann
Utrecht University
Aarti Gupta
Wageningen University
Michael Mason
London School of Economics and Political Science

BUILDING CAPABILITIES FOR EARTH SYSTEM GOVERNANCE

Jochen Prantl
The Australian National University

Ana Flávia Barros-Platiau
University of Brasilia

Cristina Yumie Aoki Inoue
Radboud University and University of Brasília

Joana Castro Pereira
University of Porto

Thais Lemos Ribeiro
University of Brasilia

Eduardo Viola
University of São Paulo and Getulio Vargas Foundation

CAMBRIDGE
UNIVERSITY PRESS

CAMBRIDGE
UNIVERSITY PRESS

Shaftesbury Road, Cambridge CB2 8EA, United Kingdom

One Liberty Plaza, 20th Floor, New York, NY 10006, USA

477 Williamstown Road, Port Melbourne, VIC 3207, Australia

314–321, 3rd Floor, Plot 3, Splendor Forum, Jasola District Centre, New Delhi – 110025, India

103 Penang Road, #05–06/07, Visioncrest Commercial, Singapore 238467

Cambridge University Press is part of Cambridge University Press & Assessment, a department of the University of Cambridge.

We share the University's mission to contribute to society through the pursuit of education, learning and research at the highest international levels of excellence.

www.cambridge.org
Information on this title: www.cambridge.org/9781009485876

DOI: 10.1017/9781108854030

First published 2024

A catalogue record for this publication is available from the British Library.

ISBN 978-1-009-48587-6 Hardback
ISBN 978-1-108-81077-7 Paperback
ISSN 2631-7818 (online)
ISSN 2631-780X (print)

Building Capabilities for Earth System Governance

Elements in Earth System Governance

DOI: 10.1017/9781108854030
First published online: January 2024

Jochen Prantl
The Australian National University

Ana Flávia Barros-Platiau
University of Brasilia

Cristina Yumie Aoki Inoue
Radboud University and University of Brasília

Joana Castro Pereira
University of Porto

Thais Lemos Ribeiro
University of Brasilia

Eduardo Viola
University of São Paulo and Getulio Vargas Foundation

Author for correspondence: Jochen Prantl, jochen.prantl@anu.edu.au

Abstract: This Element develops a new Strategic Capabilities Framework for studying and steering complex socio-ecological systems. It is driven by the central question of what are the most essential capabilities that ought to be fostered for addressing the fundamental twenty-first-century environmental challenges and Earth system transformations. The authors' objective is to innovate transformative ideas towards better climate and ocean governance that are of interest to both academics and policymakers in the field. Rather than investigating the design and effectiveness of institutions in governing the climate and the oceans, the authors offer an alternative approach starting from the assumption that global governance arrangements must be informed by the capabilities of the communities affected. This Element aims to offer out-of-the-box thinking about capabilities-focused and community-centred frameworks that align multi-level systems of governance with the fundamental challenges of global environmental change. This Element is also available as Open Access on Cambridge Core.

Keywords: earth system governance, complex adaptive systems, climate engineering, Indigenous and local knowledge systems, capabilities

ISBNs: 9781009485876 (HB), 9781108810777 (PB), 9781108854030 (OC)
ISSNs: 2631-7818 (online), 2631-780X (print)

Contents

1 Introduction

> It is not so much that humanity is trying to sustain the natural world, but rather that humanity is trying to sustain itself. It is us that will have to 'go' unless we can put the world around us in reasonable order. The precariousness of nature is *our* peril, *our* fragility.
>
> (Sen, 2013: 6, emphasis in original)

> Rather than only a global effort, it would be better to self-consciously adopt a polycentric approach to the problem of climate change in order to gain the benefits to multiple scales as well as to encourage experimentation and learning from diverse policies adopted at multiple scales.
>
> (Ostrom, 2009a: 32)

Humanity has lived through an age of acceleration since the mid-twentieth century. Natural resource overconsumption, spiralling greenhouse gas emissions that have yet to peak, loss of biodiversity, ocean acidification, and population growth have moved Planet Earth to the edge of a precipice. According to the World Meteorological Organization (WMO, 2023), July 2023 has been the hottest month on record globally, with sea ice at an all-time low and ocean surface temperature at an unprecedented high. Yet, with greenhouse gas concentrations in the atmosphere still increasing, temperature records will continue to be broken. Extreme weather events are becoming the norm. Globalization has amplified the connectivity of social systems and ecosystems and has exposed the sensitivity and vulnerability of the socio-ecological Earth system.[1] If unmanaged, this will lead to irreversible destruction of the planet's habitat.

The Covid-19 pandemic triggered 'the largest global economic crisis in more than a century' (World Bank, 2022: 26). Along with the social and political disruptions it has caused, the pandemic has thrown a spanner into the wheels of globalization and peoples' way of life. The worsening climate crisis makes future global health emergencies (Disease X) inevitable. While governments have been able to manage the symptoms of Covid-19, its underlying causes remain. To pretend there is a way back to the pre-pandemic normal is as irresponsible as insisting that Planet Earth is a crowded cruise ship with no steering wheel that is doomed to wreck. However, the interconnected climate and pandemic crises have laid bare the short- and long-term pressures on lives and livelihoods. According to a recent landmark study, humanity would need 1.6 Earths to maintain current global living standards (Dasgupta, 2021).

---

[1] *Sensitivity* is defined as the mutual effects arising from system connectivity. *Vulnerability* denotes the opportunity costs of disrupting system connectivity.

Like a telescope, the interconnected climate and pandemic crises have high-lighted the increased demands on government and governance, at the precise moment when state capacity to deliver essential services has shrunk (National Intelligence Council, 2021). Strategy and statecraft to win the war against deadly viruses and climate emergencies must struggle with an enemy that causes havoc in multiple arenas of hyperconnected socio-ecological systems simultaneously (Goh and Prantl, 2020). How can humanity sustain itself, save itself from its worst excesses, and pull away from the precipice of climate catastrophe? Are these simply questions of global governance and political will, top-down policy design, and science and technological innovations pro-vided by a small group of countries with the capability to do so? Or does this generational task require a more transformative change in thinking, a paradigm shift that opens space for polycentric approaches and greater diversity in addressing the most fundamental problems of the twenty-first century?

1.1 Aims and Objectives

This Element develops a new Strategic Capabilities Framework (SCF) for studying and steering complex socio-ecological systems. It is driven by the central research question of what are the most essential capabilities that ought to be fostered for addressing the fundamental twenty-first century environmental challenges and Earth system transformations. Our primary objective is to innovate transformative ideas towards better climate and ocean governance that is of interest to both academics and policymakers in the field. Rather than investigating the design and effectiveness of institutions in governing the climate and the oceans, we offer an alternative approach starting from the assumption that global governance arrangements must embrace polycentricity and be informed by the capabilities of the communities affected.

In this context, the rich body of literature on 'capabilities' (e.g. Alkire, 2002, 2005; Nussbaum, 2000; Sen, 1985, 1988, 1999, 2005, 2009; Stewart, 2005; Tonon, 2018) is both an inspiration and a reminder that the enhancement of both individual and collective living conditions ought to be at the centre of govern-ance processes and practices.[2] Underlying the capabilities approach are the

---

[2] Garza-Vázquez and Deneulin (2018) provide a very helpful overview of the ongoing discussion of individual versus collective capabilities. We appreciate the importance of the capability approach as an evaluation framework that focuses on individual circumstances. However, as Mary Graham (1999: 106) has observed, 'a person finds their individuality within the group'. In this Element, we depart from the ethical individualism of the capabilities approach that values communities and systems only for the capabilities they provide for individuals but not for their own functioning (Holland, 2008a, 2014). The Strategic Capabilities Framework generates explanatory leverage for Earth system governance to better understand how to generate well-being beyond an individualistic and anthropocentric perspective. Nature and people, humans and

multiple combinations of functionings that provide people (rather than markets or governments) with the agency and freedom of choice to live one way of life over another. Functionings are the items and social opportunities a person may value and have reason to value doing or being. In this context, Indigenous and Local Knowledge Systems (ILKS) provide a missing link to rebuild synergies between the well-being of people and the conservation of complex ecosystems (Lam et al., 2020; Watene, 2016). Over thousands of years, Indigenous communities have developed ways and means to embrace complexity, operating on the principle that, in order to survive, one can only consume as many resources as the natural world can sustain. Intergenerational responsibilities and justice matter too (Watene, 2013; Winter, 2022). The next generation must have equal access and equal rights to use natural resources (UNDP, 2020: 92).

Human development is conceptually founded on capabilities, revolving around the central objective of expanding people's choices and improving their well-being. Since 1990, the Human Development Report has represented the most sustained effort in translating the idea of capabilities – particularly the Human Development Index (HDI)[3] – into tangible policy recommendations. The HDI departed from the idea that economic growth should be the primary criterion to measure the development of a country. Bhutan, for example, enshrined in its 2008 Constitution Gross National Happiness (GNH) (rather than Gross Domestic Product) as a key driving principle of state policy (Gross National Happiness Commission, 2009).[4] The question of what constitutes and contributes to human development and well-being has become critically important in the age of the Anthropocene (Crutzen, 2002), as the unfolding climate and pandemic crises force us to rethink our way of life. This requires nothing less than a more integrated socio-ecological systems perspective on sustainable development: human development and ecosystem preservation targets are separable but not separate (Reyers et al., 2018).

The onset of the Anthropocene demands appreciation of, and analytical engagement with, the multiple linkages that arise from the unprecedented connectivity of socio-ecological systems (Young, 2017). Operating within planetary boundaries that must not be transgressed has become a critical challenge (Rockström et al., 2009a, 2009b; Steffen et al., 2015). Crossing

---

non-humans, are interdependent socio-ecological systems that form a collective; nature is not simply a resource humans can exploit to generate individual well-being. See Section 2.

[3] The HDI measures the average achievement in three core dimensions of human development: a long and healthy life, being knowledgeable, and having a decent standard of living.

[4] The GNH index emphasizes the importance of traditions and connection to nature. It rests on four foundational pillars: sustainable and equitable socio-economic development; environmental conservation; preservation and promotion of culture; and good governance (Gross National Health Commission, 2009: 18).

tipping points that – once triggered – lead to irreversible and far-reaching consequences for the Earth system (Lenton et al., 2008) must be avoided. On the one hand, this requires techniques and mechanisms that can be deployed when the complex system reaches a critical threshold. On the other hand, this also requires rethinking the foundations and paradigms upon which our Earth system governance arrangements are based. Engaging with the economic, political, and social foundations of societies is crucial to achieve the objectives of climate change mitigation, adaptation, and resilience (Inoue and Franchini, 2020; Pereira and Viola, 2022; Viola and Franchini, 2018). Critical engagement with the 'rational foolishness' of behavioural economics constitutes part and parcel of this exercise (Sen, 1977). Global agreement on a foundational sustainability *Grundnorm* that helps to guide sustainable development policies and practices is a necessary step in this direction (Young et al., 2017: 65–70).

In sum, the aim of this Element is to offer out-of-the-box thinking about capabilities-focused and community-centred frameworks that realign the multilevel systems of governance with the fundamental challenges of global environmental change:

1. We connect the complexity, diplomacy, strategic studies, climate, and ocean research agendas and bodies of literature.
2. We combine approaches that seem to be diametrically opposed in their objectives: that is, the calls for (a) the recovery of ILKS on how to build different relationships to nature, and (b) the development of advanced science and technology to manipulate Earth's climate.
3. We apply our analytical framework to the climate and the ocean across all levels of analysis.

Shifting the attention towards capabilities enables us to study how global governance – understood as the processes and practices of social groups and institutions, both formal and informal, to address public policy problems at multiple levels – can produce better global public goods to enhance living conditions.

1.2 The Argument

In this Element, we argue that *the enhancement of individual and collective living conditions within planetary boundaries needs to be at the centre of governance processes and practices*. We depart from the individualist approach to capabilities and advocate for a systems and communities approach at the interface of individualism, collective understandings of capabilities, and Indigenous knowledges (Holland, 2008a; Schlosberg and Carruthers, 2010).

At the same time, global governance encompasses not just one, but many worlds and multiple species encountered at the global, regional, and domestic levels (Celermajer et al., 2023; Hurrell, 2007; Inoue, 2018; Inoue and Moreira, 2016). Consequently, Earth system governance must be polycentric (Ostrom, 2009b, 2010) and adaptive (Dietz et al., 2003; Folke et al., 2005).

We substantiate our argument by reconceptualizing 'capabilities', introducing two entry points, *technology* and *ILKS*, that provide potential levers to enhance individual and collective living conditions. While the opportunities for harnessing scientific and technological innovations such as artificial intelligence (AI) are obvious, so are the risks. The world's most pressing environmental challenges will not be met without an enabling environment that helps AI fulfil its potential while mitigating the risks (World Economic Forum, 2018). Questions that need to be addressed include the following:

- What is the specific purpose of, and justification for, developing AI capabilities in addressing Earth's environmental challenges?
- What governance frameworks will regulate the deployment of new technologies?
- Who will have access to, and benefit from, innovations and inventions?

None of these questions can be answered sufficiently without probing the paradigms driving the age of acceleration (Biermann, 2021), for example the unsustainable dichotomy between the human sphere and the ecosphere. Human and non-human survival cannot be pursued separately but ought to be part and parcel of Earth system maintenance. Looked at from a capability perspective, despite declining poverty, rising economic growth, and significantly improved living standards over the last thirty years, globalization has not led to greater satisfaction and well-being. In fact, the world has seen a surge in discontent and anger (Mishra, 2017; OECD, 2021). Consequently, rather than attempting and failing to go back to pre-Covid-19 business as usual, we need to answer the following questions:

- What is the appropriate paradigm that will facilitate the survival and progress of humanity?
- If it is not the pursuit of profit and economic growth, what capabilities enhance the living conditions and the well-being of people?
- What are responsible and sustainable interventions in Earth systems under unprecedented stress (Goh and Prantl, 2020)?

The Cochabamba Statement, proclaimed in April 2010 by more than 30,000 participants from over 100 countries of the World People's Conference on

Climate Change and the Rights of Mother Earth, has recognized Planet Earth as a living being with inalienable rights that must be respected and protected.[5] As Winter (2022: 190) has observed, as a bearer of rights and dignity, Planet Earth bears subjectivity that 'assigns responsibilities to respect the freedom and interests of the subject'. Human beings are only one node within an extremely complex and interdependent socio-ecological system.

Furthermore, the Cochabamba Statement has called for the recovery and revalorization of ILKS and practices. The ILKS across the globe are most instructive in their mastery of navigating complex socio-ecological systems. Three examples illustrate our point:

1. In New Zealand, the Māori notion of *whakapapa* denotes the deep connections amongst people and ecosystems, including all flora and fauna (Brondizio et al., 2019). Well-being is inseparable from the natural world, with all human beings, non-human animals, and the natural world sharing a common past, present, and future (Watene, 2016: 292).

2. Indigenous communities in Australia emphasize their collective responsibility to look after clan or family ('the mob'). Well-being and development are directly derived from both this relationship and the transmission of knowledge and practice to the next generation. At the same time, '[t]he Land is the Law', and 'the relation between people and land becomes the template for society and social relations' (Graham, 1999: 105–106). Indigenous Australians have produced political order through a 'relational-ecological' disposition which very much differs from the understandings of political order and inter-polity relations of the academic discipline of International Relations (Brigg et al., 2022).

3. In Indonesia, the cooperative management of centuries-old rice terraces in Bali showcases how complex natural environments can be maintained in a sustainable way and enhance the individual and collective well-being of people (Lansing, 2006; Lansing and Cox, 2019). Water temples manage the irrigation of rice terraces that extend beyond villages to entire watersheds. Over hundreds of years, the cooperation of Balinese local farmers up-stream and down-stream generated optimal harvests and preserved watersheds. The farmers' capability to navigate their complex natural environment in a sustainable way exposed the limits of the 1960s Green Revolution aimed at boosting agricultural production through fertilizers, pesticides, and enhanced irrigation methods.

---

[5] See Rights of Mother Earth, Proposal Universal Declaration of the Rights of Mother Earth, https://pwccc.wordpress.com/programa/, accessed 1 July 2023.

According to the UN Human Development Report (UNDP, 2020: 185)

> [l]ocal nature-based solutions have the potential to contribute to transformational change, even at the global level – for two reasons. First, many local and community decisions can add up to substantial global impact. Second, planetary and socioeconomic systems are interconnected, and local decisions can have impacts elsewhere and at multiple scales.

Focusing our attention on the carbon sink capacity of the Amazon Basin is particularly instructive here. By preserving the storage capacity of the Amazon rainforest, on a per capita basis, Indigenous people roughly offset the greenhouse gas emissions generated per capita by the top 1 per cent of the income distribution (UNDP, 2020: 201). Indigenous peoples exercise stewardship of nature by controlling deforestation, reducing carbon dioxide emissions, living in sync with nature, and by instinctively understanding the root causes of climate change. As Fa et al. (2020) estimate, approximately 36 per cent of the world's intact forest landscapes are on the lands of Indigenous peoples.

In sum, the comparative advantage of highly diverse ILKS spread around the world is their capability to care for country and to navigate the complexities of interconnected and interdependent socio-ecological systems. While technological advances provide enormous opportunities for much-needed Earth system stress relief, Indigenous and local nature-based solutions provide as yet untapped potential for paradigm shifts in how to protect biodiversity and pursue a responsible and sustainable way of life.

1.3 Element Outline

Sections 2 and 3 outline the conceptual framework to study Earth system governance. The SCF will be introduced examining complex problems from a system perspective rather than discrete levels of analysis (domestic, regional, global). However, our framework needs to be embedded in the long-standing traditions and practices of local communities. Therefore, in a second step, the importance of ILKS and knowledge co-production will be highlighted as part and parcel of our capabilities framework.

Section 2 develops the SCF for Earth system governance, building on Strategic Diplomacy (Goh and Prantl, 2017; Prantl, 2021; Prantl and Goh, 2016; Prantl and Goh, 2022). The section identifies two key, though very different, entry or leverage points to advance capabilities in Earth system governance: technology and ILKS.

Section 3 situates the idea of many worlds-one planet in relation to the SCF. It highlights that co-production between ILKS and technology offers a critical entry point to enhance the living conditions of people in the Anthropocene by creating safe and sustainable spaces for humans and non-humans. Scholars have framed different ways of being and knowing, constituting multiple realities that stand ontologically as *other* worlds, even though they interact, conflict, and co-constitute each other. Many worlds-one planet implies that human societies create 'worlds' that entail diverse knowledge sub-systems and notions of nature. Enhancing capabilities for governance in a complex and technologically driven planet is more likely to succeed if diverse knowledge systems are not only acknowledged in processes of co-production but also fully embraced with epistemological parity. The voice and representation of the peoples inhabiting those multiple worlds, like Indigenous and local communities, are key for advancing Earth system governance processes that are legitimate, socially just, and that promote ecological and economic sustainability.

Sections 4, 5, and 6 apply the SCF to two key issue areas of Earth system governance: the climate and the ocean. While the technology and ILKS entry points seem to be diametrically opposed in their approach and located at opposite ends of the capabilities spectrum, they both offer critical insights for the enhancement of individual and collective living conditions within planetary boundaries. Taken together, the two sections allow us to engage in a conversation, establish maximum bandwidth of the respective arguments, and take stock of the comparative advantages of the chosen entry points, which will be synthesized in the concluding section.

Section 4 applies the capabilities framework to climate change, focusing on the potential, limits, and risks of technologies designed to manipulate the planet's climate – commonly referred to as *geoengineering, climate engineering*, or *climate intervention* in coping with Earth system transformations. There are two major families of climate engineering technologies: carbon dioxide removal (CDR) and solar radiation management (SRM). Advocates of CDR argue that it is necessary because of the slow pace of global carbon emission reductions. Advocates of SRM contend that it will probably become necessary in the second half of the twenty-first century as a complement to mitigation, adaptation, and CDR. Building on the well-established climate engineering literature in social science in general and global governance in particular, the section uses the technology entry point to juxtapose explicitly the novel technological aspects of the climate engineering debates with ILKS claims and insights.

Section 5 applies the capabilities framework to ocean governance. It focuses on the role of the knowledge of coastal communities – Indigenous or non-Indigenous – in addressing key problems of the oceans, in comparison with the best available knowledge produced by the scientific community and companies. Tapping into the traditional wisdom of coastal and island communities is key for coping with the rapid changes of Earth system transformations. While local communities have proved their ability to use ocean resources sustainably, they demand recognition of their rights in activities such as fishing and navigation. Technology users, on the contrary, with high-tech fishing gear, satellites, and bioprospecting methods represent the biggest risks to resource depletion and, in many ways, the solutions. Also, climate change solutions may have irreversible impacts on ocean health. The mutual recognition of, and better connection between, those two groups of knowledge producers have been a challenge since the 1992 Rio Summit.

Section 6 synthesizes the findings of the Element in light of the SCF. It fleshes out the connection between the very diverse knowledge systems of 'technologies' and 'ILKS' for better Earth system governance. The section offers steps forward for both scholars and policymakers on building better analytical and policy capabilities for addressing the twenty-first century's fundamental environmental challenges and Earth system transformations.

This is a team-authored project which started off with a disagreement over the critical capabilities required to master the challenges of earth system governance in the twenty-first century. The project is unusual, as we did not attempt to arrive at a consensus. Nor did we attempt to produce an edited volume, which would have allowed us to disengage, constructively, into our own sections. Rather, this Element offers a platform for a much-needed exchange amongst a diverse group of scholars from three different continents, with multiple voices and perspectives, organized around and facilitated by the SCF. As a team, we are searching for common ground across our contrasting views for better Earth system governance. As such, the Element is – in the best Sen (1999, 2013) tradition of letting people choose the capabilities they value – an invitation for public debate and continued reflection by a much broader audience. This Element claims to be more than the sum of its team-authored parts.

2 Re-aligning Systems, Institutions, and Communities

This section introduces a capabilities framework for Earth system governance. It identifies two key entry or leverage points in advancing strategic capabilities: technology and ILKS. In substantiating our framework, we build on central properties of the innovative framework of Strategic Diplomacy (Goh and Prantl, 2017; Prantl, 2021; Prantl and Goh, 2016, 2022) and develop a SCF that operates at the interstices of domestic, regional, and global politics. The SCF helps to address the challenge of how to generate well-being beyond both an anthropocentric perspective and an individualistic perspective (Watene, 2016; Winter, 2022). The focus is on building *collective* capabilities of nature and people, human and non-human, to navigate complex and interdependent socio-ecological systems. In doing so, we do not attempt to arrive at a predetermined list of capabilities that ought to be applied across the globe. Instead, following Ostrom's (2009a: 32) polycentric approach to climate change, we offer a *strategic* framework that has *enough* traction to facilitate the development of tailored capabilities at the domestic, regional, and global levels 'to multiple scales as well as to encourage experimentation and learning from diverse policies adopted at multiple scales'.

In the following section, we will first briefly introduce Strategic Diplomacy and then specify the core tenets of our integrated SCF.

2.1 Strategic Diplomacy

Today's most pressing security and policy challenges – great power conflict, economic dependency, climate change, and other non-traditional threats such as pandemics – are all complex problems. That is, they entail interconnectivity, non-linearity, and emergence (the system is more than the sum of its parts).

Driven by what some have called the Fourth Industrial Revolution (Schwab, 2018), contemporary global affairs are transforming in four central ways:

1. *Shrinking policy space*: The exponential speed at which these changes are happening, including their accumulated effects for countries, societies, and industries, has led to a fundamental redistribution and decentralization of power and capabilities. According to Schwab (2018: 67), policymakers 'are constrained by rival power centres including the transnational, provincial, local and even the individual. Micro-powers are now capable of constraining macro-powers such as national governments'. Whilst globalization has pushed the connectivity of socio-ecological systems to unprecedented levels, the capacity of governments, including their policy space and the reaction time to control outcomes and to deliver essential services, has shrunk (National Intelligence Council, 2021).

2. *Policy nexuses*: Policy issues are hard to isolate because they often form nexuses with a range of interconnected problems – for instance, the nexus between climate change and ocean health. At the same time, small-scale policy problems have the potential to become tipping points with large-scale, system-changing consequences.

3. *Shifting boundaries and policy frames*: The boundaries that divide individual, local, national, regional, and international action have become blurred. New boundaries are drawn comprising diverse sets of actors, which form novel assemblages and networks to govern policy issues within specialized orders or sub-systems. As a result, new public policy spaces emerge with

polycentric lines of authority that transcend the Westphalian state (Ostrom, 2010; Sassen, 2006; Slaughter, 2017).

4. *Institutional fragmentation*: Issue complexity, together with the shift and diffusion of relative power, has led to the fragmentation of global governance architectures becoming a matter of increased interest for academics and policymakers alike (Biermann et al., 2009a; Boulet et al., 2016; Kanie et al., 2017; Prantl, 2005, 2014).

Strategic Diplomacy is defined as 'the process by which state and non-state actors socially construct and frame their view of the world; set their agendas; and communicate, contest and negotiate diverging core interests and goals' (Prantl and Goh, 2016: 8). As such, it provides the capability to embrace the diverse knowledge systems available in many worlds on one planet, as discussed in the following section. The importance of knowledge and reality as being socially constructed and being socially embedded within a cultural, institutional, and historical context is well established (Berger and Luckmann, 1966; Biermann et al., 2009b; Reed, 2011). However, in a world that is in the midst of order transition, highly contested, and deeply pluralist without a single reference frame, knowledge co-production has become essential (Inoue, 2018). This is particularly true for transnational problems such as climate change or pandemics that are critically dependent on planetary ways of engagement.

Strategic Diplomacy is a diagnostic and policy framework developed for a complex operational environment that is challenged by shrinking policy space, policy nexuses, shifting boundaries, and institutional fragmentation. As a diagnostic framework, Strategic Diplomacy is a toolkit that enhances our repertoire of knowledge production, problem representation, and framing.[6] It disaggregates complexity by examining the wider domestic, regional, and global systemic environment within which policy issues are embedded. As a policy framework, Strategic Diplomacy aims at regaining and maximizing policy space.

Differing from standard accounts of 'regime complexity' (e.g. Alter and Raustiala, 2018), the Strategic Diplomacy framework is based on the important insight that contemporary international order is best understood as a *complex adaptive system*, with three key properties: interconnectedness, non-linearity, and emergence. *Interconnectedness* refers to the high degree of connectivity between the individual components of a complex system. *Non-linearity* means that there is a fundamental disproportionality between cause and effect. Minor events may create tipping points with major effects. *Emergence* denotes that new phenomena emerge from the interactions of the individual components of a

---

[6] On the importance of expanding our toolkits for navigating complexity, see Young, 2017: 223–229.

complex system, that is the whole system is more than the sum of its parts. Strategic Diplomacy takes its analytical eye off short-term events and is concerned about the long-term behaviour and structure within which policy issues are embedded. Our analytical starting point is therefore what Murray Gell-Mann has called, 'a crude look at the whole' (Miller, 2015: 4).

Forging effective strategies is essential to maximizing policy space and minimizing uncertainty. Defining and agreeing upon 'desirable' futures for our planet has become a fundamental priority for policymakers (Bennett and Satterfield, 2018; Biermann, 2018). This is easier said than done in a world that is characterized by the return of geopolitics, the inequalities of global capitalism, and backlash politics, with populism, dissatisfaction with traditional political parties, reaction against globalization, and anti-elite sentiments (Hurrell, 2018). There is no mutually agreed set of rules and principles on how societies should be organized and relate to each other. Hence, strategies – whether national, regional or global – are hotly contested. Yet practising diplomacy with a renewed emphasis on strategy is crucial, particularly because the common reaction to complexity and uncertainty is to seek refuge in oversimplification, tactics, and process.

Strategic Diplomacy consists of three key elements:

1. Diplomacy undertaken with an accentuated strategic rationale of maximizing policy space with the long-term objective of *system maintenance* or *system change*.[7]
2. The (shorter-term) diplomatic practices of contesting and negotiating conflicting strategic ideas and priorities.
3. A strategic narrative that is grounded in domestic knowledge systems and developed with the stated aim of generating buy-in from both domestic and international audiences (Freedman, 2013; Prantl and Goh, 2022).

In a nutshell, Strategic Diplomacy generates critical analytical leverage in recasting conventional analysis of well-known policy issues with the broader aim of offering different directions for policy planning. The framework is guided by the following set of questions:

1. Mapping borders: What is the wider domestic, regional, and global systemic environment, including the epistemological context, within which the respective policy issue is embedded? What are the key nodes that hold the

---

[7] System maintenance and system change are understood as Weberian ideal-types, two poles at opposite ends of a broad spectrum of possible system states or permutations. Socio-ecological complex systems do not return to the same state when they experience feedback loops and oscillate; they are dynamic and display different behaviours following each cycle.

system together? Where do we draw the boundaries of the system? Boundaries are not drawn by the system alone. As Meadows (2008: 97) reminds us: 'We have to invent boundaries for clarity and sanity; and boundaries can produce problems when we forget that we've artificially created them. . . . Where to draw a boundary around a system depends on the purpose of the discussion – the question we want to ask.' Hence, mapping borders is not just a mechanical exercise in depicting system parameters but a strategic choice of how to represent an issue.

2. Framing issues: If 'Strategic Diplomacy' is to be deployed:

   a) What is the final objective, that is the strategic *endpoint*, of system intervention?

   b) What are the most appropriate *entry or leverage points* from which to influence the system?

   c) What are the *tipping points*, if any, that may either dampen or amplify system dynamics?

3. Strategic policy: Following from the answers to questions 1 and 2, what is the most appropriate strategy to (re-)gain and maximize policy space in order to shape the systemic environment in the respective issue area? What is the most persuasive strategic narrative to generate maximum buy-in from key strategic domestic and international audiences?

The SCF that follows leverages key features of the diagnostic properties of Strategic Diplomacy, particularly its problem diagnosis, issue framing, and knowledge production features. It is a collective capabilities-generating framework, in search of intergenerational continuance. Intergenerational collective continuance can be understood as 'a community's capacity to be adaptive in ways sufficient for the livelihoods of its members to flourish into the future' (Whyte, 2013: 518). This will be discussed in the following section.

2.2 The Strategic Capabilities Framework

Both the social science and policy communities are now in broad agreement that twenty-first- century global governance and multilateralism:

- Has become more 'complex' (e.g. Alter and Raustiala, 2018; Orsini et al., 2020; Young, 2017);
- Is operating on a 'formal-informal continuum' (Prantl, 2013); and,
- Is 'messy' (Haass, 2010) or fragmented (Biermann et al., 2009a; Boulet et al., 2016; Kanie et al., 2017; Prantl, 2005, 2014).

However, two observations are in order.

First, there is a significant demand for better disaggregating of the concept and 'system effects' of complexity (Jervis, 1997; Orsini et al., 2020) and translating that into the practice of strategic policy planning and global governance (Goh and Prantl, 2017; Prantl, 2021; Prantl and Goh, 2016, 2022). Capabilities do not function in a vacuum but within a complex adaptive systemic context that must be fully understood, nudged, and nurtured.

Second, complexity thinking is particularly helpful to study and navigate systems that are neither simple nor entirely random (Young, 2017). Hence our aim to apply complexity thinking to make sense of the most essential capabilities that ought to be fostered for addressing the fundamental twenty-first-century environmental challenges and Earth system transformations.

The SCF is based on the understanding that system boundaries and framings are not a single-lane road, because the same problem can be part of multiple knowledge systems and framings, with different meanings to different people. Therefore, the question of whose boundaries and framings matter and will be taken into account is of critical importance (Leventon et al., 2021). This challenge becomes particularly evident when juxtaposing technology with ILKS. In this context, we understand technology as the development of capabilities, that is advanced technological solutions, to manipulate nature. The ILKS, on the other hand, are understood as the 'cumulative body of knowledge, practice, and belief, evolving by adaptive processes and handed down through generations by cultural transmissions, about the relationship of living beings (including humans) with one another and with their environment' (Berkes, 2018: 8). In essence, technology and ILKS are different frames and social constructions of the same world. They represent alternative ways of knowledge production and alternative ways of life (Jasanoff, 2004).

However, technology and ILKS are not mutually exclusive (Kukathas, 2010). To pose the question of *who* is for ILKS and *who* is for technology leads to a dead end. Navigating change and social transformation is the ultimate quest for two interconnected worlds: the world of global society (top-down) and the world of local community (bottom-up). In doing so, Earth system governance must ask and answer the following critical question:

> *How to tame technology that has contributed to unsustainable exploitation of natural resources, overconsumption, and socio-environmental degradation while rediscovering a way of life that is both responsible and sustainable.*

The accelerating innovation in science and technology, the Fourth Industrial Revolution, carries great potential in improving the ways of engaging with the natural environment and managing resources (World Economic Forum, 2017).

Most importantly, it provides an opportunity to reshape the interaction between social systems and ecosystems in a sustainable way. This is not just a matter of technological innovation and application, but even more so an invitation to review critically the paradigms driving our lives. Paragraph 136 of the legally binding 2015 Paris Agreement

> [r]ecognizes the need to strengthen knowledge, technologies, practices and efforts of local communities and Indigenous Peoples related to addressing and responding to climate change and establishes a platform for the exchange of experiences and sharing of best practices on mitigation and adaptation in a holistic and integrated manner. (United Nations, 2015)[8]

At the same time, Indigenous groups have been recognized as a formal constituency at UN climate change conferences since 2001. While they have not been able to participate in negotiations, they participate as observers with the opportunity to lobby parties to the negotiations. The Glasgow Climate Pact (United Nations, 2021) has reconfirmed 'the important role of indigenous peoples, local communities and civil society ... in addressing and responding to climate change, and highlighting the urgent need for multilevel and cooperative action'. Furthermore, it stresses the importance of Indigenous and local 'culture and knowledge in effective action on climate change, and urges Parties to actively involve indigenous peoples and local communities in designing and implementing climate action' (United Nations, 2021: para 93).

There is therefore a strong rationale to harness the untapped potential of ILKS in enhancing individual and collective living conditions. According to the World Bank's Climate Investment Fund, '[t]he users of traditional technologies offer a worldview that respects the environment and promotes the notion of communal ownership and responsibility for its maintenance and transfer to subsequent generations' (Climate Investment Funds, 2019: para 18). The ILKS provide deep knowledge about the environment, including its sustainable use and management.[9] They operate on a paradigm that prioritizes public goods over private goods. Knowledge is considered a common pool resource passed on across generations that transcends commercial property rights. At the core of the SCF is the objective to enhance the living conditions of people – both at the individual and collective levels by creating safe and sustainable spaces for humans and non-humans in the Anthropocene. This is the *strategic endpoint*

---

[8] Furthermore, Article 7.5 of the Paris Agreement recommends that climate adaptation 'should be based on and guided by the best available science and, as appropriate, traditional knowledge, knowledge of Indigenous People and local knowledge systems'.

[9] For example, forests and soil are not only uniquely important for local and Indigenous communities but also play an important role in carbon sequestering and storage (Climate Investment Funds, 2019: para 31).

we hold constant throughout our analysis. Furthermore, we follow Holland's (2008b) call to add Sustainable Ecological Capacity as a meta-capability that must be nudged and nurtured to enhance human and non-human well-being. We identify technology and ILKS as two *strategic entry* or *leverage points* in the SCF to realize Sustainable Ecological Capacity and to achieve the strategic endpoint (see Figure 1).

On the surface, technology and ILKS are different entry points of Earth system governance with diametrically opposed objectives. This is something we will discuss in our empirical Sections 4 and 5 with reference to climate and oceans, keeping the separate entry points as our analytical centre of gravity, while juxtaposing technology with ILKS and vice versa.

The SCF acknowledges that technology and ILKS are competing demands arising from different conceptions of order, nature and society, science and technology, and knowledge production. Yet both deserve much greater academic scrutiny. Our framework provides explanatory leverage over what we consider the key conceptual challenge:

> *How to connect the two different entry points of technology and ILKS in order to achieve Sustainable Ecological Capacity and to produce better global public goods to enhance the living conditions of people affected by climate change.*

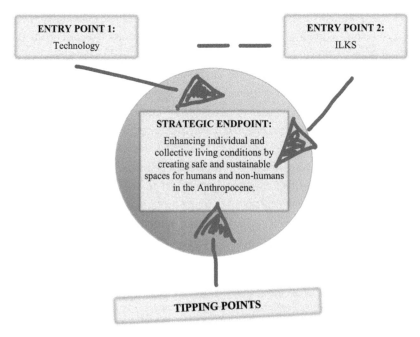

Figure 1 Key properties of the SCF

Addressing this challenge, we start from Meadows' (1999) idea of twelve places to intervene in a system. System interventions are conditioned and constrained by the capacity of entry points to elicit change in system features and dynamics. Entry or leverage points are points of power-generating system effects. System paradigms have the strongest potential for system effects, while entry points targeting the system boundaries and parameters have the weakest potential. Engaging with Meadows' tentative list of leverage points and accepting her invitation to 'think more broadly about the many ways there might be to get systems to change' (Meadows, 1999: 3), we distil five ideal-type system features that are receptive to system interventions (in decreasing order of effectiveness): paradigms, system goals, system design, feedback loops, and boundaries (see Figure 2).[10]

Paradigms. Overarching complex systems are continuously evolving worldviews and beliefs that inform single or collective action. Paradigms provide a powerful script about how the world works. It is 'the mind-set out of which the system – its goals, structure, delays, parameters – arises' (Meadows, 2008: 162). This is particularly relevant, as the mainstream paradigm of environmental policy falls short of providing solutions for the manifold challenges arising from the climate emergency unfolding within the complex socio-ecological system of the Anthropocene (Biermann, 2021).

System goals. These refer to the primary purpose or core functions of a system, understood as the trajectory, along with the *predominant* norms, values,

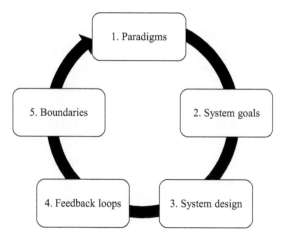

Figure 2 Entry points and potential system effects (in decreasing order of effectiveness)

---

[10] For other attempts to build on Meadows' idea of leverage points and identify system characteristics, see Abson et al. (2016); Birney (2021); Leventon et al. (2021).

and goals that a system supports. For example, economic growth and profit maximization can be seen as the emergent narrative towards which many socio-economic systems are oriented. That does not mean however that the system itself articulates its goals or that all actors within the system share these goals. System goals are, by nature, contested.

System design. This refers to the institutions and social structures that organize relationships, information flows, and self-organization within the boundaries of a system, and that trigger feedback loops. Both ecosystems and social systems can change through self-organization, adding new factors or vectors to physical or social structures, triggering new amplifying or dampening feedback loops. In ecosystems this power to self-organize is called evolution; in social systems this is called technological advance or social transformation (Meadows, 2008: 159–161).

Feedback loops. These are the dynamics arising from interactions between multiple nodes, actors, and vectors within a system. One can distinguish between *negative* feedback loops and *positive* feedback loops, which respectively dampen or amplify effects away from a system's equilibrium (Jervis, 1997: 125–176; Meadows, 2008: 25–34).

Boundaries. These are the system parameters, comprising key nodes, actors, and vectors that define a system.

Putting the SCF to work and following from the above, we show that the deployment of technology is primarily about *improving system design* and *navigating feedback loops to maintain the system and prevent system collapse.* The ILKS are mostly concerned about *the paradigms* and *system goals driving a socio-ecological system*, with potential leverage on *system design.* According to Otto et al. (2020: 2358), traditions and ILKS are important potential *social tipping points* in stabilizing the Earth climate system by 2050. In order to achieve rapid global decarbonization, *social tipping interventions* may trigger contagious system effects that are potentially irreversible and difficult to stop, resembling dynamics observed in epidemiology or social movements. Examples of social tipping interventions include the reconceptualization of economics and valuation measures, including Indigenous approaches to nature. In a nutshell, targeting system goals and paradigms have the greatest potential system effects relevant for decarbonization transformation. Looked at from a capabilities perspective, we need to address the following fundamental questions:

> *How can we utilize tipping points in triggering transformative change to maintain or improve the quality of life for people? Where do technology and ILKS feature in achieving Sustainable Ecological Capacity?*

Previous research has established that fragile systems are particularly prone to transformative change (Schellnhuber and Held, 2002). This begs the question whether our socio-ecological systems are at a critical juncture to embrace transformative change through either technology or ILKS, or a combination of both. The scale and speed of contemporary transnational challenges, along with the fragmentation in global governance, has highlighted the disequilibrium between problem-solving demands and problem-solving capacity. According to the US National Intelligence Council (2021: 3), '[t]here is an increasing mismatch at all levels between challenges and needs with the systems and organizations to deal with them. The international system ... is poorly set up to address the compounding global challenges facing populations'.

The OECD (2021) posits that there has been a global surge in public discontent since the 2008 global financial crisis, despite rising per capita GDP and wealth over the last three decades (1990–2019), sharply declining extreme poverty, and a global middle class emerging with significant improvements in living standards. This surge in discontent highlights the limits of the goals that are driving our social systems: focusing on economic growth and wealth maximization does not lead to satisfaction and well-being.

In sum, in a planetary system that is on the precipice of crossing abrupt and potentially irreversible tipping points (Lenton et al., 2019),[11] there is strong demand for new paradigms that are based on collective capabilities rather than utilitarianism. This can only be achieved by reappraising the social contract that is underlying the relationship between state, society, the economy, and the environment. In this Element we show how embracing technology and ILKS can have mutually reinforcing system effects for the enhancement of individual and collective living conditions.

Together, technology and ILKS can be considered *sustainability interventions* (Abson et al., 2016; Ostrom, 2009b) to engage with the root causes of unsustainable human development that increasingly operates outside safe planetary boundaries (Steffen et al., 2015). Those root causes include:

- the lost paradigm of people being connected with nature,
- the misalignment of system goals and safe planetary boundaries,
- ineffective institutional design governing socio-ecological systems, and
- fragmented knowledge production that tends to produce weak system interventions.

---

[11] According to IPCC (2021), unless there are immediate, rapid, and large-scale reductions in greenhouse gas emissions, limiting warming to close to 1.5°C or even 2°C will be beyond reach. Welsby et al. (2021) estimate that, in order to limit the temperature increase to 1.5°C relative to pre-industrial times, by 2050, nearly 60 per cent of oil and fossil methane gas and 90 per cent of coal must remain unextracted.

As this section demonstrates, there is a gap between the magnitude of the planetary crisis we are facing and the governance solutions we have presented so far. There is a significant demand to realign the systems, institutions, and communities that contribute to the solutions. Top-down science and technology alone cannot provide all the answers.

The SCF offers an integrated analytical and policy planning conduit to push the capabilities envelope further, with a view to realign governance sub-systems and institutions across the domestic, regional, and global levels with the fundamental challenges of Earth system transformations. However, to generate maximum leverage, the SCF needs to be embedded firmly in the long-standing traditions and practices of local communities. Therefore, in a second step, the importance and properties of ILKS and knowledge co-production will be further fleshed out as part and parcel of our capabilities framework.

3 Co–producing Knowledge in Many Worlds on One Planet

> When we tell that our river is sacred, people say: 'This is some kind of folklore', when we tell that the mountain is showing us that it is going to rain and that this day is going to be prosperous, a good day, they say: 'No, a mountain does not speak anything'.
>
> (Krenak, 2019: 26)

The climate emergency, accelerating biodiversity loss, and the deepening severity of the socio-environmental challenges now coupled with the health and economic crisis brought by the Covid-19 pandemic provide evidence that systemic changes and new forms of governance for a safe and just Earth are long overdue. As the previous section highlighted, transformative change must be thought of within a complex adaptive system that transcends traditional levels of analysis, for example the unit versus system levels of analysis[12] and there is significant demand to realign the systems, institutions, and communities that contribute to the solutions. However, we live on one planet where many worlds co-exist, and there are not one-size-fits-all solutions, which risk not only being unjust but also to fail, as the challenges are so complex and the problems so wicked that plural and polycentric governance pathways are, in our view, the only way forward.

The strategic capabilities approach identifies ILKS as one of the strategic entry points to achieve the objective of *enhancing the living conditions of people – both at the individual and collective levels – by creating safe and sustainable spaces for humans and non-humans in the Anthropocene* (strategic endpoint), or, put differently, recognizes that multiple knowledge systems

---

[12] For further information, see Prantl (2021).

inform governance capabilities. The twelve places of intervention proposed by Meadows (1999) and adopted here were distilled into five ideal-type system features that are receptive to system interventions (in decreasing order of effectiveness): paradigms, system goals, system design, feedback loops, and boundaries (see Figure 2). These offer leverage points to get systems to change (Meadows, 1999: 3).

As technology alone cannot elicit change in system features and dynamics necessary to achieve the strategic endpoint, ILKS should be considered part and parcel of this Element's capability framework. Beyond the temptation of managerial, technocratic, and top-down 'solutions', we consider that multiple and plural voices must be heard. Therefore, there is a need to level the playing field, changing existing spaces or creating new ones for knowledge co-production through processes that consider both technology and ILKS as entry points in parity. This does not mean that they are equivalent, nor that alone they can have the systemic effects necessary, but that they should be considered on equal terms. Ontological and epistemological parity should happen in co-production processes towards the strategic endpoint detailed in this Element. Our proposition is that diverse agents with diverse knowledge systems could then be involved in knowledge co-production and co-creation of pathways that leverage systems change.

As scholars attempt to unpack multiple ways of being and knowing, which can be ontologically considered 'other' worlds, they face a challenge to develop new frames that, on the one hand, recognize the planetary challenges of living on a 'new Earth' (Biermann et al., 2009b; Crutzen, 2002; Nicholson and Jinnah, 2016; Röckstrom et al., 2009b), and, on the other, take into consideration the existence of many worlds that interact, conflict, and co-constitute each other (Inoue, 2018; Inoue et al., 2020; Inoue and Moreira, 2016; Ling, 2014; Onuf, 2013; Tickner and Blaney, 2012).

In this direction, we need to question our theories and concepts and how they are constitutive of our worlds. It is important to expose our 'world-political' conceptions because they situate what counts or not, what is part of our world and our time, or what/who is excluded (Blaney and Tickner, 2013: 9). For Tickner (2013), understanding this is not the same as epistemological relativism, neither is it a 'post-truth' world or a way of denying the importance of scholarship and science, but assessing to what extent our notions empower or exclude actors and themes, making them invisible, marginal, or absent from public debates and scientific research (Forsyth, 2014). Therefore, it is necessary to be open to *'other possible worlds or forms of life that are represented as implausible, ideological, or spurious, and so often consigned to the realms of fiction, fantasy, or nonsense'* (Blaney and Tickner, 2013: 9), or even declared as non-existent or illegitimate (Smith, 2012: 103).

This section explores how the idea of knowledge co-production, co-creation, and dialogues between ILKS and technology can provide entry points to leverage change mainly, but not exclusively, on paradigms, system goals, and system design. These are considered as places for systemic intervention. The relationship between different knowledge systems – in this Element, technology and ILKS – is complex, and this section aims to help navigate this complexity within the SCF.

We argue that co-creation of knowledge and solutions between ILKS and technology could foster system effects and changes in paradigms, system goals, and system design. In this sense, knowledge co-creation based on epistemic parity (technology and ILKS as significant entry points) should be the means for systemic change, increasing the possibilities to achieve the strategic endpoint. For co-creation to occur, processes must be inclusive and just, while Indigenous peoples and local communities are considered agents in knowledge co-production. Consequently, the list of essential capabilities to address fundamental environmental challenges and Earth system transformations can account for multiple conditions and circumstances, for humans and non-humans (Holland, 2021).

Knowledge co-production has two meanings. The first implies that knowledge is co-produced in and through society, constituting the world (Jasanoff, 2004), and, as such, it is an intrinsic element of governance (Molen, 2018: 19). At the same time, knowledge co-production has become an aspiration in sustainability science (Miller and Wyborn, 2020) in the sense that claims for more inclusive and diverse spaces for co-production have become common. These two meanings are interrelated as understanding that the co-constitutive dimension of knowledge (world-making) is a step to recognize and open-up to other worlds.

We suggest that a polycentric 'many worlds on one planet' approach to Earth system governance implies recognizing that human societies create 'worlds' that entail diverse knowledge sub-systems and notions of nature. Enhancing capabilities for governance in a complex and technologically driven planet is more likely to succeed if different knowledge systems are acknowledged in processes of co-production. In terms of the SCF, it is a matter of recognizing the interconnectedness and complementarity between the two entry points to promote system change. The voice and representation of the people inhabiting multiple worlds are key for advancing Earth system governance processes that are legitimate, socially just, and that promote ecological and economic sustainability for humans and non-humans. This section draws on a literature review and document analysis on ILKS and knowledge co-production, with a focus on the ontological and epistemological dimensions. It is divided into three sections.

First, we discuss why it is necessary to recognize multiple knowledge systems in Earth system governance, based on the assumption that knowledge and society are in a mutually constitutive relationship. Following that, we present what is knowledge co-production based on a many worlds-one planet perspective to highlight the nexuses between knowledge co-production and Earth system governance. The third section attempts to synthesize and present ILKS and co-creation as an essential part of the capability framework – as one of the entry points necessary to provoke changes in paradigms, system goals, and design.

Our conclusion is that although international norms already recognize Indigenous knowledge, and there are some practices of knowledge co-production, like the ones which have been occurring in the Intergovernmental Science-Policy Platform on Biodiversity and Ecosystem Services (IPBES) and the United Nations Framework Convention on Climate Change (UNFCCC), more research is needed in order to assess the extent to which these processes of co-production happen with ontological plurality and epistemological parity and to what extent they are able to constitute per se entry points towards systemic change.

As a consequence, we also suggest that there is a need to create more fora for knowledge co-production and to develop a research avenue on how to co-produce knowledge considering all actors as peer agents in an ontological and epistemologically plural, equitable, and just context. The capabilities approach is one possible path (Bockstael and Watene, 2016), but it is important to consider its limitations regarding the focus on human agency and on dignity, the need to have cross-cultural conversations with Indigenous and local communities, and the importance of relational approaches to nature to bridge the gaps between ILKS and Western development thinking (Watene, 2016).

3.1 Parity among Multiple Knowledge Systems

> *Scientific knowledge, in particular, is not a transcendent mirror of reality. It both embeds and is embedded in social practices, identities, norms, conventions, discourses, instruments, and institutions.*

(Jasanoff, 2004: 3)

Cornell et al. (2013: 61) define knowledge systems as broader than science. They are made up of 'agents, practices, and institutions that organise the production, transfer, and use of knowledge'. In the IPBES glossary,[13] knowledge systems are defined as

---

[13] See www.ipbes.net/glossary?f%5B0%5D=title_az_glossary%3AK. Accessed 26 October 2019.

[a] body of propositions that are adhered to, whether formally or informally, and are routinely used to claim truth. They are organized structures and dynamic processes (a) generating and representing content, components, classes, or types of knowledge, that are (b) domain-specific or characterized by domain-relevant features as defined by the user or consumer, (c) reinforced by a set of logical relationships that connect the content of knowledge to its value (utility), (d) enhanced by a set of iterative processes that enable the evolution, revision, adaptation, and advances, and (e) subject to criteria of relevance, reliability, and quality.

The IPBES definition is broader than that of Cornell et al. (2013), though they share common points. We share with them the understanding that knowledge systems have multiple actors engaged in a specific domain, in dynamic and interactive formal and informal processes.

Biermann et al. (2009b) assert the importance of considering the social construction of knowledge, the cultural and temporal embedding of the researcher, and the reflexivity of social knowledge because of the normative uncertainty that prevails in the governance of the global environment. In this sense, we should acknowledge that science has been a fundamental source of awareness about socio-environmental degradation and the planetary limits to economic growth. For Pádua (2002: 28), science can be associated with the origins of environmental thought not only in the context of the consequences of the great urban–industrial transformations that began in Europe at the end of the eighteenth century but also with other historical processes, among which he emphasizes European colonial expansion and the incorporation of large regions of the planet into a world-economy under its dominance, including biomes and ecosystems that were not part of the Western historical experience.

On the other hand, science is a culturally specific knowledge system that is intrinsic to modernity. As such, it has been premised on the modern dichotomies as subject/object, nature/society, norm/fact, based on a paradigm of knowledge as a product of a subject–object colonial relationship (Quijano, 1992). Jasanoff (2004: 2–3) argues that the ways in which we know and represent the world are inseparable from the ways in which we choose to live in it. Thus, it is important to highlight the mutually constitutive relationships between society and knowledge, which means that society cannot function without knowledge, the same way as knowledge cannot exist without appropriate social support, and to recognize how political and social factors influence science and vice versa (Forsyth, 2014: 220).

The paradox is that science has been part of the problem and the solution of the planetary socio-environmental crisis. Science and technology derived from it have been part of the historical and socio-economic processes that foster production and consumption patterns related to socio-environmental degradation. At the same time, science as an authoritative mode of knowledge has been providing evidence of global environmental damages to the Earth system, and many solutions have come from technology. However, the crisis has become systemic and, we argue, the only way forward is going beyond science and technology. In this sense, the concept and practice of knowledge co-production, which engages different knowledge producers – agents, processes, and institutions (Cornell et al., 2013 and IPBES, 2019)[14] – can contribute to enlarge the SCF.

Escobar (2016: 21) highlights that a One-World World (OWW) has been enacted through epistemological practices and historical choices that have as a landmark the 'Conquest of America' and a

> two-fold ontological divide: a particular way of separating humans from nature (the nature/culture divide); and the distinction and boundary policing between those who function within the OWW from those who insist on other ways of worlding (the colonial divide). These (and many other derivative) dualisms underlie an entire structure of institutions and practices through which the OWW is enacted.

For Escobar, global climate change is evidence of the OWW's crisis, the same as the 'ubiquity of the language of crisis to refer to the planetary ecological and social condition', and the struggles for mountains, landscapes, forest, and territories that appeal to relational and pluri-ontological understandings of life (Escobar, 2016: 21–22), all underscore the need for change. In Escobar's view, knowledge produced in these struggles is more far-sighted and appropriate in the current crisis context that, on the one hand, evidence the need for civilizational transitions, and, on the other hand, is profoundly affected by planetary dynamics featured by the Anthropocene (Escobar, 2016: 23–24).

The great acceleration of the Anthropocene means that social-ecological systems interact more rapidly and frequently in our globalized planet causing accelerated planetary socio-environmental change. There are calls for innovative ways to define and conceptualize the challenges and to search for solutions for the present and the future. However, there is a gap between the magnitude of the challenges and the governance solutions that have been presented so far. In this context, there is greater demand to connect knowledge systems in the search for alternative pathways for humanity (Tengö et al., 2014). Science is intrinsic to governance (Molen, 2018) and essential in responding to the planetary crisis, but it cannot be seen as a neutral tool to explain and control the world *out there*, and, by itself, cannot provide all the answers.

---

[14] See www.ipbes.net/glossary?f%5B0%5D=title_az_glossary%3AK. Accessed 26 October 2019.

Moreover, considering how the Anthropocene departs from the stability that humanity has long experienced in the Holocene, we need to engage with epistemological and ontological questions. As human impact on Earth is so great that no place on the planet can be considered as untouched or 'natural', scholars are pointing to the conceptual end of nature, to a post-nature world, and to hybrid concepts to refer to the nature–society relation in non-dichotomous ways (Leis, 1999; Rudy and White, 2014: 129; Wapner, 2010, 2014). In this sense, the notion of pluriverse (Escobar, 2016) is an important contribution.

Escobar points out that there are multiple worlds or ontologies (Escobar, 2016: 13). There are multiple 'reals' in contrast to the assumption of a single reality with multiple cultures, perspectives, or subjective representations, but not in the sense that a pluriverse view should 'correct' the OWW view of a single real, as 'a truer account of 'reality'' (Escobar, 2016: 22). The pluriverse proposal of multiple reals is non-dualist, thus is not an either/or view of a pluriverse versus a universe.

Our argument calls for parity among different knowledge systems in ontological and epistemological terms. In this direction, we call for envisioning (the establishment of, the promotion of) processes for knowledge co-creation among diverse knowledge systems, as the case of the two entry points in the SCF. This argument does not entail equivalence between ILKS and technology, but calls for participation of actors who have typically been excluded and the recognition of their knowledge systems as entry points in the proposed framework.

Accordingly, we concur with the worldism notion that social diversity and conceptual abundance are as significant as analytical rigour and methodological parsimony in scientific inquiry. In that view, multiple worlds refer to distinctions and connections (Ling and Pinheiro, 2020: 320). Their model of dialogics or 'chatting' is based on the Daoist yin/yang dialectics, in which the engagement across and within 'subaltern' worlds is enabled by

> revealing opportunities for discursive agency (relationality), by recognizing political solidarity from disparate voices at disparate sites (resonance) and by developing ethics with compassion as a guide to action (interbeing). (Ling and Pinheiro, 2020: 318)

Relationality is premised on ontological parity, positing that social power takes place despite structural inequities. In this sense, everything and everyone, even the smallest, should be considered equally significant. It acknowledges power relations, interrogates silences but also asks 'how the silenced talk back not just speak up'. Resonance invites attention to 'creative transformation combined with respect for local knowledges' and it is based on the notion of musical vibration or how 'we may hear the common song arising from disparate voices in disparate places'. Finally, interbeing means acting ethically and with compassion as two indissociable principles and treats the 'Self as a reverberative subjectivity ("I am because of you, you are because of me")' (Ling and Pinheiro, 2020: 322).

Dialoguing with ILKS, and considering them in epistemological and ontological parity with academic knowledge, is a move in the direction of more inclusive understandings of knowledge that can help us to reconceive and reconcile the nature–society relation. This move is important not because these knowledge systems are useful (as a resource), nor because of Indigenous peoples' closeness to nature (eco-Indigenism), neither due to an 'anti-scientific' attitude, but because Indigenous and local populations are legitimate agents and through their active participation, their ways of knowing and of being on the planet can contribute to different understandings of Earth politics in the Anthropocene (Nicholson and Jinnah, 2016).

The first step, presented by Escobar, is the recognition of multiple reals in a non-dualist manner. The next step is creative listening and speaking (CLS) as the method proposed by Ling and Pinheiro (2020) to put worldist chatting in practice. It will be further elaborated in the next section. The ontological and epistemological parity are not measured by an attributed value of different knowledge systems or the potential scale of the solutions informed by them, but on the acknowledgement of multiple entry points that makes us more far-sighted in our search for innovative thinking with equity and justice implications.

3.2 Knowledge Co-production and Many Worlds

It is necessary to promote respectful and equitable dialogue and connection across different knowledge systems for improved policy and governance, supporting mechanisms for learning, and decision-making (Tengö et al., 2014: 584, 589). The literature on knowledge co-production has its origins in at least three different academic fields: public administration, science and technology studies, and sustainability science; though these fields portray different views on co-production, they share a constructivist basis (Miller and Wyborn, 2020).

Instead of focusing on co-production as a de facto reality, sustainability science has turned it into a normative aspiration: 'science should be co-produced with its users' (Miller and Wyborn, 2020: 90). However, turning knowledge co-production into an aspiration cannot become a panacea or a checklist of who is present in a meeting, as such a view risks overlooking the unequal power relations and procedures that co-produce knowledges and societies (Miller and Wyborn, 2020). In fact, understanding that knowledge is always co-produced is a first step to acknowledge that some spaces of knowledge production are considered more legitimate than others and that some actors have unequal access to spaces and processes where scientific/academic knowledge is produced.

We suggest that it is possible to consider co-production critically as a de facto reality, and, simultaneously, to aspire to build new and inclusive arenas to allow for processes to produce knowledge jointly. In the SCF, it requires parity between technology and ILKS as entry points. In this sense, knowledge co-production can be defined as the engagement of different knowledge producers (agents, processes, and institutions) for the production of knowledge (based on Cornell et al., 2013 and IPBES, 2019),[15] normally, for a specific domain and with three main stages: joint problem framing, knowledge integration, and experimentation (Cornell et al., 2013: 63).

Tengö et al. (2017: 20) propose the multiple evidence-based approach to co-produce knowledge and engage with different knowledge systems. This approach considers that knowledge systems are incommensurable, and recognizes power asymmetries between them, the flow of knowledge, and credibility (Cornell et al., 2013: 61). Such ideas can be related to the notion of *pluriverse*, as an ontological starting point for recognizing that reality (or realities) is constituted by many worlds (ontologies, ways of being in the world, experiencing it, and knowing reality) and while being interrelated, each world exists on its own (Escobar, 2016; Querejazu, 2016) and in a non-dualist relationship (Escobar, 2016).

Accordingly, CLS as a worldist method based on relationality, resonance, and interbeing calls for the creation of 'third spaces' or venues for engagement, where one can momentarily put into brackets polarized positions like the powerful versus the powerless, or the rich versus the poor, allowing for mutuality to develop and the emergence of 'other ways of thinking and doing, being and relating', despite structural asymmetries (Ling and Pinheiro, 2020: 323).

In this context, other ways of knowing, which are sometimes considered as myths or non-rational stories, need to be considered with another gaze. Taking this one step further, we should demystify the Western (European) belief that the great commercial, political, philosophical, and scientific accomplishments result from the sole effort of Europeans: 'Europe was periphery to Asia before the Christian age, and it benefited from innumerous discoveries of the Orient' (Ramos, 2013: 21–22 free translation).

We would add to this assertion that the so-called progress is as much a result of colonial exploitation as it is of 'encounters' with others. For Smith (2012:

---

[15] See www.ipbes.net/glossary?f%5B0%5D=title_az_glossary%3AK. Accessed 26 October 2019.

61), who writes from the perspective of Maori Indigenous people, knowledge and culture were part of imperialism, and '[k]nowledge was also there to be discovered, extracted, appropriated and distributed' in organized and systematic processes. The contributions of these other knowledge systems to the foundations of Western research, however, are normally neglected, since they are considered as objects of research (Quijano, 1992), not as equivalents, due to power asymmetries and prejudices that put them in ontologically and epistemologically inferior positions (Smith, 2012: 63–64).

As Cesarino (2013: 19) reminds us, 'myth' can be seen as a notion created within the Greco-European tradition to refer to other peoples' knowledge systems, to categorize what falls into the horizon of 'irrationality', in contrast to the attempt to achieve 'logos' and the monopoly of truth.

Thus, epistemological and ontological parity among worlds and knowledge systems is an essential move to enlarge the borders of our academic disciplines and a first step towards knowledge co-production processes that include traditional and Indigenous ways of knowing.

For that to happen, it is important to build and recognize spaces and fora where diverse actors are in parity, all of them having voice and agency, with due recognition of quality, reliability, relevance, and attention to incommensurabilities, which are not necessarily opposite positions. There is also a need to differentiate between (a) integration of knowledge, (b) parallel approaches to developing synergies across knowledge systems, and (c) co-production of knowledge (Tengö et al., 2014: 582). Integration refers to processes that attempt to incorporate components of one knowledge system into another through a validation process based on the latter system. A parallel approach looks for complementarities while presupposing validation across knowledge systems, each system is considered legitimate within its context with its own strengths. Each one pursues knowledge in parallel, enriching one another. Co-production of knowledge is a mutual process of knowledge generation that engages the actors in the process at all stages, including validation.

In our view, either parallel approaches or knowledge co-production are valid ways to join Indigenous peoples, traditional populations, and non-Western knowledge holders with scientists and academics. Integration presupposes or reinforces a hierarchy, which is exactly the idea that should be overcome. For instance, there is evidence that Indigenous knowledge has only been recognized in some fora, like the UNFCCC, when it validates mainstream knowledge and world perspectives (Belfer et al., 2019).

Indigenous peoples can contribute with 'holistic, embedded and bounded in the local' non-dichotomous knowledge, which values the community, has moral significance, and does not separate nature and culture, or subject and object, humans and non-humans (Inoue and Moreira, 2016: 13). This recognition needs to go many steps ahead of the traditional (neo)colonial integration and be based on co-constitution and equitable positions between multiple knowledge systems.

3.3 ILKS as Entry Point for Systems Change

Indigenous knowledge and its value has been recognized by international law and as such it should be respected, preserved, and maintained. There are international rules of Free Previous Informed Consent (FPIC) as of International Labour Convention No.169 and Mutually Agreed Terms as of the Nagoya Protocol that regulate activities involving Indigenous peoples. Environmental and development practitioners and academics have called attention to how Indigenous knowledge can be useful for governing natural resources and for ecosystem protection, conservation, and sustainable use. This is also recognized by international regimes and organizations like the Convention on Biological Diversity, the Convention on Desertification, and by the World Bank (Martello, 2001).

However, Martello (2001) warns against the view of ILKS being considered as 'resources', asserting that the language of international organizations about traditional knowledge can reflect a view of it being an 'extractable resource' in need of refining and standardization to be comprehensible, useful, and valuable (Martello, 2001: 131). This approach has also been described by Smith (2012) as being colonialist and echoes Quijano's (1992) criticism of non-Western knowledges being considered as objects, and not subjects. Martello (2001) argues that such a view establishes a 'one-way-dynamic' from the local to the international with little involvement of Indigenous and local communities.

We believe that epistemological parity is fundamental to uncover actors made invisible by previous approaches and to hear other voices in the process of co-producing knowledge about Earth system governance – an entry point to system change at the paradigm level, but also with impact on goals, design, feedback loops, and boundaries. It is noteworthy that the effort to recover ILKS within the academy may presume that it can be effectively transferable to an institution. However, this is a wrong approach (integration) as it carries the risk of viewing this knowledge system as a resource to be extracted (Agrawal, 1995; Smith, 2012; Wilson, 2004).

Smith (2012: 111–126), for example, presents the formation of a field of Indigenous research, based on Indigenous concepts, practices, and Indigenous peoples as researchers and objects of research, in what she calls the 'modern indigenous peoples' project', which goes 'beyond decolonisation aspirations of a particular indigenous community ... towards the development of global indigenous strategic alliances' (Smith, 2012: 112). Agenda-setting is a power demonstration and, in this case, also provides some evidence of self-determination. In this direction, we again suggest that knowledge co-production is not solely about the development of parallel research agendas, but jointly produced agendas.

Moreover, there is the risk of being essentialist by not considering how knowledge systems interact and relate to each other. As pointed out, there are always encounters, co-constitution, interconnectedness, and incommensurabilities. Cultures are not closed and peoples are dynamic. Agrawal (1995: 421) argues that '*neo-indigenistas*' rely on the same type of dichotomous worldview as the modernization theorists, seeking to create two categories of knowledge (Western and Indigenous) based on a few distinguishing characteristics, but forgetting the diversity and heterogeneity within each of them and that they are not separated and static, fixed in time and space. They interact and change. Thus, it is important to avoid dichotomies such as scientific and non-scientific Indigenous knowledge (Agrawal, 1995: 424; Jackson, 2011). In this sense, studies on Indigenous knowledge cannot be archived in national or international centres as databases, as resources to be extracted (Agrawal, 1995: 420).

Having these caveats in mind shows how difficult it is not to fall into the traps of essentialism, extractivism, simplification, naturalism, or co-option. One way to try to avoid these limitations is by identifying Indigenous struggles and listening to Indigenous voices and to recognize the 'situatedness' of our own work and the power struggles related to it.

More importantly, on the one hand, this is a claim for recognition of ILKS, to recognize 'how they know what they know' (epistemology and ontology), and for a change in power relations. On the other hand, Indigenous peoples in North America, the Andean region, and the Amazon in South America, Aboriginal and Torres Strait Islanders from Australia, and Māori people from New Zealand claim that they have their ways of 'coming to know' (Cajete, 2000; Kopenawa and Albert, 2013; Ramos, 2013; Viveiros Castro, 2004), and that these should be valued on their own terms (Smith, 2012; Wilson, 2004). Thus, the recognition of ILKS in epistemological and ontological parity with Western knowledge systems is a part of Indigenous struggles.

Tengö et al. (2014) point out that the power inequities and epistemological differences between diverse knowledge systems are brought to the fore in knowledge policy processes. Agrawal (1995: 431–432) presents some implications of these differences, arguing that the issue of Indigenous knowledge must be reframed as one of change in power relations and control over the use of lands and resources, including the right to decide on how to save, to use, and who can use their knowledge. This goes beyond rights over territories, or rights to keep their cultures, beliefs, practices, or capabilities to function, but resistance to a particular ontological occupation, that of the 'universal world of individuals and markets that attempts to transform all other worlds into one' (Escobar, 2016: 21). For Escobar, Indigenous, Afrodescendant, peasant, and poor urban communities' struggles are ontological struggles for many worlds.

In the case of the SCF, the struggles for the recognition of many worlds impact the definition of the strategic rationale, the identification of agents (human and non-human), the understanding of policy stages, knowledge (co-) production processes and fora, and the time frame of what is considered the short and long term. Accordingly, our proposition of knowledge co-production brings up power considerations within the SCF, because it is based on an understanding of ontological plurality and epistemological parity. The SCF should be premised on relationality. If actors are peer agents in the process of co-producing knowledge, it is necessary to explore 'third spaces' guided by resonance and interbeing (Ling and Pinheiro, 2020). Concretely, that means to create new places for co-producing knowledge (*ex ante* focus) and to look for existing processes and places where knowledge has already been or could be co-produced (ex post focus).

The Earth System Governance Project's[16] new Science and Implementation Plan states that to recognize other ways of knowing implies a transdisciplinary research effort, which is seen as a means to 'structure research process that accounts for diverse perspectives on the problem and proposed solutions by tackling the relevance that these have – as an epistemic value – for the problem and context in question' (ESG Project, 2018: 83). Such an effort should foster processes for co-design of research agendas and knowledge co-production. Concretely, that should be translated into the creation of new opportunities for collaboration, as well as building capacity and skills, but also being more creative and investing in experimentation (ESG Project, 2018: 84).

In addition, knowledge co-production with Indigenous and other local populations, who hold traditional knowledge, can surpass the domain-specific framing, dichotomies, and dualities, and provide functionalities that go beyond problem analysis, involving system understanding.

The recent Glasgow Climate Pact,[17] from COP 26, has reconfirmed 'the important role of indigenous peoples, local communities and civil society … in addressing and responding to climate change, and highlighting the urgent need for multilevel and cooperative action'. How this recognition will be

---

[16] See www.earthsystemgovernance.org/. Accessed 26 December 2020.

[17] See https://unfccc.int/sites/default/files/resource/cop26_auv_2f_cover_decision.pdf. Accessed 17 December 2021.

translated into action is yet to be seen, since most of the eight references to Indigenous and local peoples are related to ex post measures (loss and damage, protection and conservation of ecosystems to deliver essential services, and collaboration towards the attainment of the Convention objectives).

There are multiple examples of knowledge co-production with Indigenous and local populations on different issues. The IPBES established the thematic assessment of pollinators, pollination, and food production, and the Plan of Action on Customary Sustainable Use of Biodiversity under the Convention on Biological Diversity (Athayde et al., 2016; Tengö et al., 2017). Norton-Smith et al. (2016) assessed the climate impacts on Alaskan Native and American Indian tribes, including tribal approaches to climate change. Nevertheless, for Belfer et al. (2019) Indigenous participation in the UNFCCC currently lacks meaningful recognition, with power and resource inequities, despite the establishment of the Local Communities and Indigenous Peoples Platform.[18] Moreover, research is needed about the relations between the capabilities approach and ILKS (Bockstael and Watene, 2016), as well as about co-production between technology and ILKS based on relationality, resonance, and interbeing as guiding principles.

The last call of the Glasgow Climate Pact regarding Indigenous and local peoples is more in tune with our proposition, with emphasis on 'the important role of Indigenous peoples' and local communities' culture and knowledge in effective action on climate change' with an urge to parties to 'actively involve Indigenous peoples and local communities in designing and implementing climate action' (paragraph n.66 of the Glasgow Climate Pact).

It is not possible to have a blueprint of how to co-produce knowledge considering many worlds, nor to assess critically if ongoing co-production initiatives have been carried out considering epistemological parity and equity among agents. The examples of IPBES, UNFCCC, and ILO Convention No.169's FPIC evidence a need for more research to identify the challenges, shortcomings, and successes and whether these have been entry points for system change.

Relationality, resonance, and interbeing can be complemented by the principles stated by Miller and Wyborn (2020: 92), when building knowledge co-production spaces: inclusiveness and accommodation; attentiveness to how power is accorded, how the less powerful can insist on participation rights and the significance of their ways of knowing, and how processes and objectives of co-production can work to include or exclude; and, finally reflexiveness about forms and arrangements related to credibility, legitimacy, and accountability.

---

[18] See https://lcipp.unfccc.int/. Accessed 27 May 2023.

3.4 Conclusion

In this section, we have argued for the recognition of local and Indigenous peoples and their knowledge systems and suggested knowledge co-production among diverse knowledge systems and agents as a potential pathway for system change. We consider that these can be an entry point towards achieving the strategic endpoint of enhancing individual and collective living conditions in safe and just spaces for humans and non-humans in the Anthropocene (Figure 1). This entry point can leverage change on paradigms, systems goals, and design, which inform and produce alternative research agendas, problem framings, and methodological choices in a more just and equitable manner.

The starting point for this argument was the SCF. However, we pointed out that power considerations should be taken-up in the SCF as power asymmetries have prevented voices from being heard. This entails levelling the playfield and reconfiguring unilinear notions of knowledge and power based on the CLS principles: relationality, resonance, and interbeing (Ling and Pinheiro, 2020). In practical terms, that means to question and to reflect on the way we have been producing and validating knowledge, and how knowledge constitutes our worlds. This step is important to recognize and to be open to other ways of knowing beyond a mere integration approach with (neo)colonial roots. Taking a many worlds-one planet perspective means that all the actors should be considered as peer agents in relationality, through knowledge co-production or parallel approaches that look for synergies (Tengö et al., 2014) and resonance. In this direction, there is a need to create more inclusive processes and places, 'third spaces' (Ling and Pinheiro, 2021). This perspective calls for dialogue or connection (Tengö et al., 2014) with Indigenous and other knowledge systems.

In this section, we also pointed out the risks of essentialism, extractivism, simplification, co-option, and naturalism and the need to acknowledge incommensurabilities and the diversity and heterogeneity in ILKS, avoiding dichotomies as scientific and non-scientific Indigenous knowledge. Knowledge systems are not static and fixed, they interact and change across time and space (Agrawal, 1995; Martello, 2001; Smith, 2012; Wilson, 2004). So ILKS and co-production need to be framed not only as a change in power relations, the control over territories and resources or rights to keep cultures or capabilities but above all as resistance to a particular ontological occupation (Escobar, 2016). In this sense, Indigenous struggles involve the recognition of their knowledge systems and Indigenous participation as peer agents in knowledge co-creation processes.

Indigenous knowledge has already received formal recognition in international norms, but it remains difficult to achieve practical directions. There are, however, developments within the IPBES, the UNFCCC, and within academia (see Smith, 2012) which need further scrutiny.

We consider that a potential many worlds-one planet research avenue for ESG scholars could be to identify and further assess if and how knowledge co-production initiatives like the above mentioned in IPBES, the UNFCCC, and the ILO Convention No.169 actually happen, to what extent they are inclusive and accommodating, if power relations are acknowledged and the playing field is levelled in terms of participation, validation, and joint construction of problems and solutions, and how reflexive these processes have been (Miller and Wyborn, 2020: 92). Such an avenue opens the possibility for humility and for creatively confronting our current planetary crisis with plurality towards the enhancement of the living conditions of humans and non-humans.

Finally, this section argues for an encompassing capabilities framework that fosters new processes and fora for knowledge co-creation that are legitimate, socially just, and that promote ecological and economic sustainability. The debate around potential, limitations, risks, and the encounter of different knowledge systems around technologies designed to manipulate the planet's climate intentionally in the next section is a possible field for our argument.

4 Climate Governance

Climate change is accelerating and its impacts increasing. The CO_2 atmospheric concentrations and global temperatures are reaching record-breaking highs (WMO, 2020). The continuing worsening of the climate crisis evidences the failure of three decades of multilateral state efforts to fight the threat of climate change (Pereira and Viola, 2020), and prospects for the future are highly uncertain. There is currently a profound gap between, on the one hand, the mitigation pledges submitted by parties to the UNFCCC under the 2015 Paris Climate Agreement and the trajectory of policies since the signing of the agreement, and, on the other hand, the ambitious climate action needed to comply with the temperature goals agreed in Paris and to deliver a climate-safe future (CAT, 2021). Consequently, and as observed by Pasztor (2017: 419),

> [f]or many experts the question is no longer whether the world can keep the temperature rise below the goals stipulated in the Paris Agreement, but by how much will the world miss that target and how long will the overshoot last.

In this context, many are increasingly considering the role that unconventional or disruptive technologies could play in helping humanity address the climate crisis. As shall be seen, this idea has been, and will most likely continue to be, the subject of deep controversy and heated debates, not only as a result of the technical, ethical, and political challenges those technologies raise but also because the prospect of their deployment 'evokes deeply held beliefs about the proper place and role of humans in the order of the cosmos' (Carr, 2018: 66); beliefs that are embedded in traditional Indigenous cosmologies, religious beliefs, and some secular philosophical worldviews. This section thus focuses on the potential limits and risks of technologies designed to manipulate the planet's climate intentionally – commonly known as 'geoengineering', 'climate engineering', or 'climate intervention' – while juxtaposing them with traditional and Indigenous insights and claims. In addition, the section reflects upon some of the roles of Indigenous peoples and other local communities (IPLC) in combating climate change, and the challenges they face. By doing so, it illustrates the notion of the pluriverse addressed in the previous section and shows that neither top-down technology nor IKLS alone can achieve the endpoint of enhancing the living conditions of people in the Anthropocene; as previously argued, both are necessary strategic entry points for navigating the challenges of the new geological epoch.

4.1 Climate Engineering Proposals: A Brief Overview

Climate engineering proposals are commonly divided into two main categories: (a) CDR, also referred to as negative emissions technologies (NETs) or remediation technologies, and (b) SRM, also referred to as albedo modification or solar geoengineering, the former category referring to techniques designed to remove CO_2 from the atmosphere and the latter to techniques oriented to cool the Earth by modifying the reflectivity of the planet. Examples of the main proposals within both categories are summarized in Table 1.

CDR addresses the root cause of anthropogenic climate change and can be seen as a subset of mitigation (Heyward, 2013). Some of its options 'fall under the category of *geoengineering*, though this may not be the case for others, with the distinction being based on the magnitude, scale and impact of the particular CDR activities' (IPCC, 2014: 119). In turn, SRM would be like a palliative, as it is not designed to alter the concentration of greenhouse gases (GHG) in the atmosphere, but to lower the temperature rapidly by reducing the amount of energy from the sun that is absorbed by the planet. Consequently, SRM techniques would not contribute to reversing pressing problems such as ocean acidification, which can disrupt marine ecosystem functioning; additionally, SRM could trigger unintended environmental effects, such as changes in the

Table 1 Summary of main climate engineering proposals

CDR	• Reforestation/Afforestation • Bioenergy with carbon capture and storage (CCS) • Enhanced weathering (land) • Enhanced weathering (ocean) • Ocean fertilization • Direct air capture and sequestration
SRM	• Surface albedo modification (urban/desert) • Marine cloud brightening (MCB) • Stratospheric aerosols injection • Space reflectors • Cirrus clouds manipulation[19]

Source: Elaborated by the Authors based on Royal Society (2009) and NRC (2015a, 2015b)

hydrological cycle and precipitation patterns at a global scale (Doney et al., 2009; NRC, 2015b; The Royal Society, 2009).

Given its potential high effectiveness and affordability, stratospheric aerosol injection (SAI) is the most debated SRM technique; however, there are still significant uncertainties on the potential impacts of SAI deployment, including, for example, the risk of ozone depletion, negative impacts on agriculture in different regions of the world, modification of monsoons with impacts on food supply, or a decline in solar energy production due to sunlight reduction (NRC, 2015b; The Royal Society, 2009). Marine cloud brightening, another proposed SRM technique, which would imply enhancing cloud-condensation nuclei concentrations to increase cloud reflectivity and lifetime over parts of the ocean, could also have heterogeneous effects over different regions, induce changes in weather patterns with impacts on major climate cycles such as the El Niño oscillation, or disturb marine ecosystems with effects on fish availability and cloud formation mechanisms. Other SRM techniques have been much less discussed, either because of their expensiveness (e.g. space reflectors) or low effectiveness and affordability (e.g. urban albedo modification), or because not enough is yet known about them (e.g. cirrus clouds manipulation) (NRC, 2015b; The Royal Society, 2009).

---

[19] This technique implies the thinning of cirrus clouds to reduce either their heat trapping capacity or their removal, which would have a cooling effect on the planet. According to the IPCC AR5 glossary, although not strictly speaking SRM, this technique can be related to SRM. A more appropriate category to frame cirrus clouds manipulation (CCM) would be, for example, Radiation Management (Rickels et al., 2011).

CDR techniques are generally seen as less risky but more expensive (except for reforestation and afforestation) and having a much slower temperature response, requiring massive global efforts to produce measurable climate effects. It should be noted, however, that some CDR options have also been associated with major planetary risks – for example, ocean fertilization could affect the marine food web and fisheries of different ocean regions, stimulate the production of neurotoxins that could harm many marine forms of life and even humans or change the biogeochemistry of the oceans in a way that could neutralize the climate positive effect of the uptake of CO_2 or even trigger the release into the atmosphere of substances harmful to stratospheric ozone. Land management approaches, such as reforestation and afforestation, although ready for deployment with a broad understanding of risks, have relatively limited potential. Carbon capture and storage technologies are the basis of bioenergy production with carbon capture and storage (BECCS) and direct air capture and sequestration (DACS) proposals. They are designed to collect CO_2 through chemical processes (in the case of BECCS, for example, at power plants where biomass is burned for electricity, and in the case of DACS by scrubbing CO_2 directly from ambient air) and then transport and store it underground in geological reservoirs. In addition to risks of leakage and induced seismicity, much more technological development is needed to improve CCS reliability and make it economically viable to scale up globally. The BECCS in particular adds to the equation all the well-known challenges associated with bioenergy/ biofuels, including resource requirements for growing crops (e.g. water and fertilisers), additional emissions from transportation, and, as shall be seen in the next section, trade-offs with food production, natural habitats, and biodiversity. The DACS, in turn, adds the question of high costs (NRC, 2015a; The Royal Society, 2009). Other CDR techniques include enhancing natural rock chemical weathering reactions that trap atmospheric CO_2 into new stable products by, for example, 'spreading large amounts of pulverised silicate and/or carbonate minerals onto warm and humid land areas ... or onto the sea surface' (Bach et al., 2019: 2–3) – to have a significant impact, these processes would require large energy inputs for mining, processing, and transportation, but could be beneficial in reducing ocean acidification by increasing alkalinity and could impact positively on agriculture by improving crop yields and preventing erosion; however, many potential side effects are still understudied (Bach et al., 2019; NRC, 2015b; The Royal Society, 2009).

The implementation of these methods and techniques raise significant ethical and political issues that have been the subject of numerous debates over the past years. The next section turns to them.

4.2 The Ethics and Politics of Climate Engineering: A Contested Terrain

Some argue that climate engineering, particularly the SAI technique, could be used as a temporary measure to protect the planet against the effects of dangerous climate change while buying time for effective mitigation policies (MacMartin et al., 2018). The 'buying time' argument is also used by ecomodernists, who envisage a future where breakthrough technological innovation (e.g. technologies to manipulate matter freely at the molecular level) frees humanity from its dependency on the Earth's fragile ecosystems and makes universal prosperity possible. As such revolutionary technologies may not be available for many decades, climate engineering, and SRM in particular, would allow us to live through the meantime, without compromising the right to development of the poorest (Karlsson, 2020).

It is also frequently argued that if confronted with dangerous, unmitigated climate change, humanity should opt for SRM implementation. That would be the lesser of two evils, especially given the facts that deployment may be necessary to mitigate tensions arising from such a scenario and that the most adverse effects of accelerated climate change would affect the world's poorest the most – consequently, implementation would help the most vulnerable, thus being a moral imperative and a humanitarian act (Keith, 2013; Lawrence and Crutzen, 2017; Parson, 2017a, 2017b). However, it is uncertain whether such claims are true, as there are, as seen in Section 4.1, many unclear side effects associated with deployment (Hulme, 2017). Moreover, those effects could become a source of conflict (Rabitz, 2016). States which would have been negatively affected by the use of the SAI technique, for example, could demand compensation or retaliate. In addition, as SAI could be implemented at a relatively low cost, minilateral climate engineering action is a plausible possibility (Zürn and Schäfer, 2013).

The potential negative side effects related to implementation of climate engineering technologies such as SAI could outweigh the benefits of rapid and easy deployment (Ott and Neuber, 2020). Additionally, some argue that calculations of the economic benefits of deploying SAI usually ignore the expensive costs associated with the required equipment to ensure protection against violent civil protesters, cyberattacks, or warfare (Lockley, 2019), which leads us to another commonly voiced criticism against the use of the SAI technique, that is the possibility of a termination shock. If SAI was deployed as a substitute for ambitious mitigation policies, the concentration of GHGs in the atmosphere would continue to rise; if for some reason, such as social or political turmoil or a natural disaster, aerosol injection into the atmosphere was stopped abruptly, the consequences would be catastrophic. Some of those who consider the possibility of deployment wrongly assume that states would have the capacity to implement, control, secure, and terminate SAI. However, that capacity is uncertain. As observed by Zürn and Schäfer (2013: 266), climate engineering is trapped in a paradox,

> which consists in the circumstance that exactly those technologies that are capable of acting fast and effectively against rising temperatures at comparatively low costs, are also the technologies that are likely to create the greatest amount of social and political conflict.

In fact, the real prospect of implementation could aggravate tensions between the North/China and many developing countries, as the latter could accuse the former of continuing to skip their mitigation and financing responsibilities while making risky technological decisions whose potentially dangerous impacts would be felt more intensely by the world's poorest populations and middle-income countries, which have contributed the least to climate change. For these reasons, some Indigenous communities, for example, reject the humanitarian argument in favour of deployment (ETC Group, 2018). Here, the question of intentionality would be fundamental, as those who would be deploying climate engineering techniques would be doing so with the unequivocal intent of modifying the climate, knowing the risk of triggering potentially worse effects than those associated with uncontrollable global warming. Climate engineering would make the weather attributable to somebody (Corry, 2017). The tensions arising from such a scenario could further undermine the necessary multilateral climate cooperation on mitigation and adaptation. It should also be noted that the risk of exacerbating existing disagreements is made further relevant by the marginalization of developing countries in knowledge production and the insufficient inclusion of their concerns into existing scientific assessment reports (Biermann and Möller, 2019). Accordingly, there is a 'security hazard' associated with the implementation of technologies such as SAI – 'in an attempt to gain security against future risks, new technologies can create security problems that compromise the original aim of preventing risk' (Corry, 2017: 301). Consequently, even if, as some argue, the possibility of a termination shock is being overplayed within climate engineering debates, as there would be numerous ways of preventing it (see, for instance, Parker and Irvine, 2018; Rabitz, 2016), the possibility of a security hazard raises another significant ethical challenge – confronted with unmitigated climate change, future generations would be forced to choose between continuing to operate SAI, with potentially negative side effects, or accepting accelerated climate change and suffering its destructive impacts (Ott and Neuber, 2020).

Despite all the risks and uncertainties, given the gravity of the climate crisis and the insufficiency of the remaining options available, over the past few years the research community on SRM has shifted from proposing it as an emergency 'Plan B' in case of sudden climate warming, to see it as a complementary tool to mitigation, adaptation, and advocating for CDR to be used in the second half of the century. Yet, as a consequence of the passive stance adopted by most governments towards the issue, there are no explicit regulations to govern SRM. The field is being loosely, spontaneously governed by a mix of international agreements designed for other purposes (e.g. the Convention on the Prohibition of Military or Any Other Hostile Use of Environmental Modification Techniques, the Convention on Biological Diversity (CBD), and the Convention on the Prevention of Marine Pollution by Dumping Wastes and Other Matter (the London Convention)) and by the scientific community (Talberg et al., 2018).

Regarding CDR implementation, and afforestation and BECCS in particular, there are critical, still poorly recognized issues to consider when debating the ethics and politics of those proposals. Relying on land for tackling the climate crisis implies significant trade-offs with environmental and biodiversity protection and social justice goals, as even in more optimistic mitigation scenarios afforestation and BECCS are scaled up to a level that could both significantly reduce natural lands, which would impact on biodiversity, and the availability of productive agricultural land, thus raising food security concerns, and compromise traditional livelihoods; it could also conflict with local water consumption needs (Dooley et al., 2018). In addition, scenarios compatible with the temperature targets of the Paris Climate Agreement depend partly on the use of afforestation and BECCS, but investments from the private sector are still too low and no institutional or governance structures for dealing with CDR implementation exist (Fuss et al., 2016). Implementing BECCS globally, for example, will require a sharing of responsibilities between states and the design of institutional arrangements that can incentivize and monitor biomass production, energy generation, and carbon storage. Additionally, as large-scale deployment of BECCS could exacerbate the problem of land competition – peasant and Indigenous lands, in particular, may be grabbed and exploited for climate engineering experiments and deployment – political coordination and global governance of land are of the utmost importance (Minx et al., 2018).

Regarding socio-ecological justice issues associated with CDR, Morrow et al. (2020) stress that decisions on implementation must be based not only on each project's carbon capture capacity and associated financial costs but also on its potential impacts on people and nature as well as on transparency, so that the social and environmental burdens associated with such projects do not fall on those who are least responsible for the climate crisis. For Brack and King (2020: 1), the sustainable development and deployment of CDR technologies requires 'abandon[ing] the assumption … that BECCS is the pre-eminent carbon removal solution, and analyse it alongside all other … [CDR options], on the basis of full lifecycle carbon balance … as well as other ecosystem and sustainability co-benefits and trade-offs'.

Since the availability of CDR within climate models displaces some mitigation, an implicit, rather than actual, policy bet on those technologies risks creating a future need for ever increasing large-scale implementation that, if feasible, would have significant risk–risk trade-offs, and, if not, would create path dependencies and lock in worse climate-related harms. In fact, there is substantial scepticism regarding projections assuming, for example, a doubling of the current global land emissions sink by the end of the century, an expectation that 'may greatly overestimate our collective ability to manage carbon cycle flows, thereby risking doing more harm than good' (Minx et al., 2018: 21). This leads us to another point of contention in the academic literature on climate engineering.

For some, the belief that humanity can manipulate the global climate is hubristic and dangerous. It is based on eco-managerial aspirations and excessive technological optimism; a belief that objectifies the Earth, fails to recognize humanity's intellectual, physical, and moral limitations, and underestimates the highly complex, unpredictable, and potentially uncontrollable nature of socio-ecological systems as well as our fragility and vulnerability to natural phenomena – to put it briefly, the idea that the climate can be engineered lies upon the too bold assumption that humans can fully dominate the planet (the 'super agency' of the human) (ETC Group, 2018; Hamilton, 2013). Burke and Fishel (2019), for example, draw attention to the intertwinement between the social and the natural worlds, and to the unintended, unpredictable, and uncontrollable effects arising from human interference with the Earth system's fundamental processes – in other words, to the fact that power and agency are not limited to humans, but rather distributed across assemblages of human and non-human actors. As a result, '[h]umans now have influence without control, agency without power; they create effects that escape their immediate intent, or were not even imagined, which then turn back on them' (Burke and Fishel, 2019: 97). Humanity should thus think and act more humbly and cautiously. This debate is also frequently infused with ethico-spiritual concerns – while for most advocates of climate engineering the human species is an exceptional one and there are no limits to human development and expansion, and large-scale climate interventions are simply one more step in the long, ongoing process of technological evolution that has defined our development as a species, for its opponents manipulating the climate constitutes a transgression of humanity's proper limits, a violation of nature's integrity, an abomination, amounting to playing God (ETC Group, 2018; Thiele, 2019). Some religions and Indigenous cosmologies suggest a separation between the land, which is seen as the domain of the human, and the skies, which belong to the gods (Donner, 2007).

In the 'Hands Off Mother Earth' manifesto against climate engineering, Indigenous peoples ask for a recognition of their cosmovisions and inherent rights, 'including the right of Self Determination to defend their communities, ecosystems and all life from geoengineering technologies and practices that violate the natural laws, creative principles and the Territorial Integrity of Mother Earth and Father Sky' (ETC Group, 2018: 6). They also call for a serious consideration of alternative models and scenarios for achieving the temperature goals of the Paris Climate Agreement, and the inclusion into debates and decision-making of other sources of knowledge and experience, including their own – a point to which we will return in the next section. On the opposite side of the debate, late environmentalist James Lovelock (2019) believed that the planet would soon be entering a new epoch, the Novacene, in which the exponential growth of technology – artificial intelligence in particular, with super intelligent cyborgs overtaking humans – would help humanity overcome the ecological crisis (see also, for instance, WEF, 2017).

Critics also argue that climate engineering depoliticizes the climate crisis, being a 'techno-fix' for a political and social problem, and that it promotes authoritarianism; deployment, particularly of the SAI technique, would risk democracy, as governing and decision-making processes would need to be centralized and could easily be controlled by engineers and climate scientists, which would reduce political accountability and the space for ideological contestation, and limit the possibilities for political and societal transform-ation (ETC Group, 2018; Hulme, 2014). In other words, the use of climate engineering technology risks reproducing the unequal power relations that prevent us from encountering new possibilities of knowing and being on the planet; as argued in Section 3, knowledge and society are in a mutually constitutive relationship. Arguing against such criticisms, Horton et al. (2018: 7), for example, assert that the idea that climate engineering endangers democracy is based on the flawed assumption that 'a technology possesses inherent political attributes that predetermine how it enters into and reshapes social and political life'.

The debate on the potential and risks of climate engineering illustrates how technology can be both part of the problem and the solution to the crises of the

Anthropocene, hence the need to enlarge our capabilities by acknowledging multiple entry points to address the challenges we face.

In light of all the potential risks and associated controversy, more recent work has focused on how to make SRM feasible, morally acceptable, or just. For example, Grasso (2019) draws attention to the imperative of including the ideals of legitimacy and procedural justice as well as considerations of international and intergenerational distributive justice into governance as a means to increase public participation and thus minimize the risk of technocratic or elite domination, and ensuring an equitable allocation of burdens and benefits associated with deployment. Svoboda et al. (2019) discuss the human rights challenges related to climate engineering, arguing that research and potential implementation must be guided by insights and frameworks of the human rights realm. Whyte (2018), in turn, points to the fact that existing discourses on the ethics and justice of climate engineering in general are not entirely salient to at least some Indigenous peoples, as they fail to deal with issues pertaining to colonial domination and other forms of oppression that are at the heart of their struggles, and which play a central role in exacerbating climate vulnerability. Consequently, a conversation on climate engineering that obscures the topic of Indigenous self-determination limits any possibility of widespread Indigenous endorsement of those technologies. These arguments take us back to the previous section's discussion on epistemological parity and knowledge co-production via joint problem framing, knowledge integration, and experimentation as means to empower marginalized communities as well as emancipating those who represent transformative sustainability paradigms and can contribute different understandings of how to live in the new geological epoch (Pereira and Terrenas, 2022).

The next section looks in more detail at the issues mentioned above and addresses the role of IPLC in providing climate change mitigation solutions.

4.3 IPLC and Climate Change Mitigation: Potential and Challenges

Despite the minimal contribution of IPLC to climate change, their communities are among the most affected by its adverse impacts. These peoples' livelihoods are highly dependent on local biological diversity and ecosystem services; their identity, socio-economic and cultural systems, and ecological knowledge are intricately connected to their environment and lands. They often inhabit fragile ecosystems, such as tropical forests, that are located predominantly at economically and politically marginal regions. Many IPLC are among the most marginalized, impoverished, and vulnerable communities in the world, often lacking access to resources and political and institutional support to assist them in their efforts to cope with environmental shifts resulting from a changing climate, which aggravates their vulnerable condition. Climate change not only threatens the livelihoods of IPLC, it also risks the erosion of Indigenous social and cultural life and the loss of traditional knowledge (Nuttall, 2012). However, IPLC have been struggling for recognition as more than victims of climate change; they aim to be seen as agents of environmental conservation and key actors in the quest to mitigate climate change, a claim that is inextricably linked to their struggles for autonomy and land tenure rights as well as recognition of ILKS (Cuffe, 2021; Etchart, 2017). As seen in Section 3, the issue of ILKS is about empowerment (i.e. changing power relations).

Land is both a source of GHG and a climate change solution – between 2007 and 2016, agriculture, forestry, and other land use accounted for nearly a quarter, and sequestered approximately a third, of global anthropogenic emissions (IPCC, 2019). Forests and other nature-based solutions to climate change mitigation could provide approximately 30 per cent of the CO_2 reductions that are needed by 2030 to help ensure that global warming is kept below 2°C (Seddon et al., 2019). In the land sector, curbing deforestation and forest degradation has been identified as the measure with the largest potential for reducing GHG emissions; regarding carbon removal, when 'using best practices in appropriately managed landscape systems that allow for efficient and sustainable resource use and supported by appropriate governance mechanisms', reforestation of degraded land, for example, has been associated with positive socio-environmental impacts (IPCC, 2019: 29). The IPLC play an important role in this domain. The forests of the Amazon, Canada, western Siberia, South-East Asia (Indonesia, Borneo), north-west North America, and the Congo basin are major sources of irrecoverable carbon (i.e. the carbon that must not be released into the atmosphere if humanity is to reach net-zero emissions by mid-century); nearly a third of irrecoverable carbon is managed by IPLC (Noon et al., 2022) and their knowledge and practices 'bring insights of great relevance for ecosystem governance, as in controlling deforestation, reducing carbon dioxide emissions, understanding climate change and sustaining and restoring resilient landscapes' (UNDP, 2020: 34). These actors' contributions to climate change mitigation could be strengthened with the implementation of land tenure security policies (IPCC, 2019; Noon et al., 2022).

A large, growing body of literature indicates that securing Indigenous/local tenure has beneficial impacts on forest management; there is mounting scientific evidence that the outcomes associated with local forest management are as good or outweigh those for areas administered by the state or private entities, including protected areas (see the literature review by Seymour et al., 2014). For example, across the Amazon, more than 90 per cent of Indigenous land was a carbon sink between 2001 and 2020; in Brazil, Bolivia, and Colombia, the average annual deforestation rates of the period 2000–2012 in Indigenous territories were two to three times lower than in land not managed by Indigenous peoples, and estimates indicate that through forest land tenure security, those three countries could respectively avoid the emission of nearly thirty-two, eight, and three $MtCO_2$ per year (Veit, 2021). Large, well-managed community lands that are secure and protected display low deforestation rates and capture more carbon than disturbed forests; moreover, securing community land has been identified as a cost-effective climate solution, and would enable the preservation, development, and transfer of traditional knowledge within and between different communities worldwide (CIF, 2019; Veit, 2021). The contribution of Indigenous peoples to carbon storage 'is an example of how local decisions and nature-based solutions can add up to substantial easing of planetary pressures' (UNDP, 2020: 201). Securing community land and supporting forest management by IPLC are both complementary and alternative measures to deployment of climate engineering CDR techniques that would reduce our future implementation needs of those technologies and, as a consequence, the risk of trade-offs with social justice goals and biodiversity protection. At the same time, Indigenous relational and eco-centric values are a powerful basis to inform the development and use of technology in a safe and ethical manner, and help societies address the root causes of climate change and the degradation of the planet's ecosystems. As observed in previous sections, traditions and ILKS are important potential social tipping points for transformative change towards sustainability (Pereira and Terrenas, 2022).

Agroforestry, sustainable land management, and the protection of coastal ecosystems for disaster risk reduction are examples of nature-based solutions by IPLC that contribute to human development, ecosystem integrity, and climate change mitigation. Agroforestry provides sustainable livelihoods for small farmers, ensures food security, preserves and increases biodiversity, maintains soil fertility, and plays an effective role in removing and storing CO_2 from the atmosphere (UNDP, 2020; see also Bernal et al., 2018; De Stefano and Jacobson, 2018). Sustainable land management increases community resilience and ensures the continued availability of food, water, and other natural goods, while safeguarding the ability of tree species to regenerate, enhancing carbon sequestration and storage. The protection of coastal ecosystems for disaster risk reduction mitigates the impacts of extreme weather events on human settlements, supports unique and rich ecosystems and biodiversity, and preserves stored carbon (UNDP, 2020). To be applied as effectively as possible, and ensure local benefits, these and other practices should be improved through adequate policies that make practical and constructive use of local community input, combining traditional knowledge and modern science, as 'traditional knowledge alone may be insufficient to address climate change even in regions where it has proven effective' (CIF, 2019).

These examples show ILKS's potential to provide answers to the climate challenges we face (IPCC, 2022). To scale-up nature-based solutions, empowering locally led action that is built on respect for the rights of IPLC and holding international and regional consultations aimed at compiling information on best practices that can inform global action are key. The strengthening of local actors depends on legal rights frameworks, devolution of responsibilities and budgets, capacity building, consistent application of safeguards in planning and implementation, and collaboration mechanisms (UNEP, 2022). These mechanisms point to the importance of strong institutions and public authorities capable of enforcing legal frameworks and upholding IPLC's rights of access to their traditional territories, alongside dialogue spaces wherein stakeholders, including vulnerable and powerless actors, produce regulations to prevent over accumulation of land and over exploitation of natural resources (Gabay and Alam, 2017).

It is important to note, nevertheless, that the roles and potential contributions of IPLC to climate change mitigation have been highly undervalued by most societies (UNDP, 2020). The literature on how to mobilize traditional knowledge for mitigating climate change is still sparse, as the importance of traditional knowledge in tackling the problem has only recently been recognized (CIF, 2019). Additionally, despite some advances in recent years, Indigenous peoples are still often sidelined at global climate conferences (Cuffe, 2021) and few international climate funds directed towards land tenure and forest management reach communities on the ground, with international NGOs, development agencies, and consulting firms receiving the bulk of the resources available (Davis et al., 2021; Veit, 2021). Most importantly, the vast majority of the world's community land is either not formally recognized in national laws or is held by communities under customary tenure arrangements, which makes their territories vulnerable to expropriation for predatory economic activities. As global demand for commodities intensifies, land disputes between IPLC, on the one side, and governments and companies, on the other, and territorial encroachment from illegal actors are becoming more frequent and growing more dangerous; murders of Indigenous and other environmental and human rights defenders are on the rise (Pereira and Viola, 2022; Veit, 2021). Aggravating the situation further, protections for IPLC have been dismantled by governments around the world through the implementation of policies designed to boost economic recovery in the context of the Covid-19 pandemic (Dil et al., 2021).

Land tenure insecurity makes IPLC more vulnerable not only to dispossession for extractive activities and to climate change impacts but also to climate engineering CDR projects such as large-scale afforestation and BECCS, and nature-based solutions like protected area expansion, which frequently intersect with the territories of IPLC. Policies and projects that are implemented without collaboration or the consent of the affected communities can create significant local opposition as, in many cases, such actions are perceived as 'carbon colonialism' and a threat to land rights. At the same time, failure to recognize the role that communities on the ground play in climate change mitigation and to invest in the capacity of IPLC to develop their own 'culture-and-nature-based solutions' – including carbon removal activities – on their lands significantly limits the potential for building critical synergies between local well-being, ecosystem conservation, and the mitigation of climate change, and promoting transformative change (Townsend et al., 2020; Tugendhat, 2021).

We saw earlier in this Element that at the twenty-sixth Conference of the Parties (COP) of the UNFCCC more than 140 countries accounting for over 90 per cent of the world's forests signed the Glasgow Leaders' Declaration on Forests and Land Use, committing to halt and reverse forest loss and land degradation by 2030. The Declaration recognizes that meeting global land use, climate, biodiversity, and sustainable development goals requires support for IPLC (UK Government and United Nations Climate Change, 2021a). Within this context, a few developed countries and eighteen funders collectively pledged to invest $1.7 billion to assist IPLC in their efforts to protect biodiverse tropical forests (UK Government and United Nations Climate Change, 2021b). This is a step in the right direction. However, as previously seen, in the absence of mechanisms to ensure that funds reach communities on the ground, it is unrealistic to expect that international assistance leads to transformative change and improved local well-being; a new, bottom-up global climate finance framework is needed (Davis et al., 2021). Moreover, few climate pledges under the Paris Climate Agreement explicitly acknowledge the contributions of IPLC and fewer yet include land tenure security and support to local forest management as important measures to achieve CO_2 emissions reductions (Veit, 2021). It should also be noted that the Glasgow Declaration is vaguer than the 2014 New York Declaration on Forests, under which forty countries pledged to halve natural forest loss by 2020 (United Nations Climate Summit, 2014), a target that was missed by a large margin. There is still a long way ahead. Notwithstanding recognition of IPLC's culture and knowledge, the UNFCCC has historically focused on climate technology progress, hence the need for spaces wherein knowledge and solutions are co-produced between ILKS and technology.

The quest for a safe climate future is full of challenges, uncertainties, and controversies. Yet there is at least one certainty: if climate engineering and other technological solutions to climate change are to contribute to the enhancement of individual and collective living conditions in the Anthropocene, they must be considered alongside the roles, well-being, and rights of IPLC, connecting worlds and knowledge systems to look for alternative pathways for humanity.

5 Ocean Governance

Covering about 71 per cent of the Earth's surface, the ocean is a giant set of multiple ecosystems connected to land and the atmosphere. Amongst the services it provides are temperature regulation and carbon storage; thus, it is considered a critical planetary support system (IOC, 2020; IPCC, 2019). Despite that, ocean science is still an underdeveloped discipline compared to life sciences (Levin and Poe, 2017; Polejack, 2022) and to geopolitics (Jones, 2021; Sullivan and Cropsey, 2018). The growing importance of the so-called blue economy and related issues revolving around ocean environmental protection and resource management has pushed maritime security to the top of the agenda of major global security actors (Bueger and Edmunds, 2017). This was accompanied by calls for a much more substantial treatment of maritime security in the academic discourse, including calls to move beyond 'seablindness'. Sullivan and Cropsey (2018: 2) define seablindness as the failure of states to recognize 'the oceanic foundation of their commerce and security'. While state authorities and private companies have used technologies to explore marine mineral and biological resources further, traditional and local communities have become increasingly threatened by large-scale economic activities. Looked at from the perspective of IPLC, two lessons stand out: they do not know seablindness, and they do not necessarily perceive the ocean as the victim of human activities; on the contrary, the ocean provides for their livelihoods. As such, IPLC consider the ocean both as the cradle of life and the saviour of humanity. Consequently, protecting the ocean means protecting their livelihoods and protecting humankind at the same time.

The IPLC knowledge, practices, beliefs, and fears have led to a relationship with the ocean that may be considered very different from state and market-led initiatives. New Zealand's Māori, for example, use *whakapapa* as their 'genealogical connections' to the universe (Rameka, 2018). Andean communities from Peru, Bolivia, and Chile worship *Pachamama* (Mother Earth). Those systemic and intergenerational relationships also have implications for how younger generations learn about their responsibilities and how 'future generations' matter in building capabilities (Watene, 2013). Capabilities involve both the short term and the long term. At the same time, connecting the individual, community, and systemic levels across time and space is critical for capability building.

Countries have recognized different communities formed by their own history and culture, as was discussed in multilateral meetings such as the Earth Summit in 1992. Concerning the ocean, Indigenous people and local communities usually live close to mangroves or other fragile ecosystems which they have taken care of over several generations. Mangroves, for instance, are excellent carbon sinks and should remain commercially unexplored. However, the recognition of communities within the national territory does not mean they are autonomous and sovereign, despite the calls of the 1992 Earth Summit. For example, Article 8 j of the 1992 UN Convention on Biological Diversity commits the contracting parties, as far as possible and as appropriate, and subject to their national legislation, to

> respect, preserve and maintain knowledge, innovations and practices of indigenous and local communities embodying traditional lifestyles relevant for the conservation and sustainable use of biological diversity and promote their wider application with the approval and involvement of the holders of such knowledge, innovations and practices and encourage the equitable sharing of the benefits arising from the utilization of such knowledge, innovations and practices.

In the same vein, the 2023 Biodiversity Beyond National Jurisdiction Treaty (BBNJ)[20] recalled the United Nations Declaration on the Rights of Indigenous Peoples and local communities in its preamble. In Article 5, on general principles and approaches, it calls for '[t]he use of relevant traditional knowledge of Indigenous Peoples and local communities, where available'. The BBNJ text mentions Indigenous peoples thirty-three times and local communities thirty-one times. It also mentions climate seven times, enabling a broader pathway for the treaty implementation process.

What are the implications for ocean governance? Apprehending 'communities' from these different perspectives and exploring how they intersect (or not) with each other, and decision-makers at the national, regional, and multilateral scales, is of critical importance. While communities contribute to the formation of complex socio-ecological systems (Levin and Poe, 2017), they do not necessarily have a voice in national and multilateral arenas. Even though the UN GEO 6 (Global Environmental Outlook Report, 2019) has shed light on

---

[20] Draft agreement under the United Nations Convention on the Law of the Sea on the conservation and sustainable use of marine biological diversity of areas beyond national jurisdiction (advanced, unedited PDF). www.un.org/bbnj/.

some aspects of their existence and interests, IPLC participation in the World Trade Organization, Food and Agriculture Organization (FAO), UN Development Program (UNDP), and UN Environment Program (UNEP) is hardly comparable.

In some recent cases, Small Island Developing States (SIDS), Pacific Small Islands Developing States, and Caribbean Islands (CARICOM) have been participating in key multilateral talks such as the biodiversity and climate regimes, as well as the BBNJ treaty negotiations. Yet, this has not been the case in other regimes related to shipping, fishing, tourism, and geopolitics in general. Furthermore, deep-sea mining is a completely different case, since Nauru, Tonga, Cook Islands, and Jamaica signed exploration contracts with the International Seabed Authority (ISA).[21] They are individual small island countries working with high-technology stakeholders.

For the ongoing treaty-building negotiations within the ISA, IPLC are usually either invisible or dependent on diplomats of like-minded countries and other authorities.[22] In fact, one of the most challenging political issues is the representation of minorities and local stakeholders in national decision-making processes. As curious as it may seem, IPLC leaders often need to travel abroad to call the attention of international stakeholders in order to get some visibility in their own country. This is the classical 'boomerang effect' as described by Keck and Sikkink (1998). Therefore, even if IPLC have some voice at the local level, they struggle to be heard at the domestic and multilateral scales. Sustainable or community fisheries arrangements are generally the most frequent examples worldwide.

Global governance involves many worlds from the local to the global levels, with different knowledge systems (Hurrell, 2007; Inoue, 2018). Consequently, there is indeed a need to build more inclusive processes and spaces, a need to facilitate ontological plurality and epistemological parity, as discussed in Section 3. We argue in this Element that the enhancement of individual and

---

[21] There were twenty-two contractors and thirty-one contracts in July 2023. www.isa.org.jm/exploration-contracts/. Accessed 14 July 2023.

[22] Concerning the ocean, there were two treaties under negotiation in 2023: The International Seabed Authority 'Mining Code' and the Biodiversity beyond National Jurisdiction Treaty (BBNJ). They were expected to be open for signature in 2020, but negotiations were postponed because of the Covid-19 pandemic. The BBNJ has a final text that was open for signature in 2023. Concomitantly, the Treaty on the Prohibition of Nuclear Weapons (TPAN) entered into force in January 2021 with the support of NGOs. The TPAN is interesting for our debate for three reasons. First, existing nuclear weapons are sufficient to kill all forms of life on Earth, but participation in multilateral negotiations was a privilege for senior diplomats and army officers. Second, many nuclear tests were carried out in the deep ocean, but the damages of radioactivity are still underexplored. It shows how the ocean was used as a 'free place to destroy' and how islanders and marine life were removed from their islands or ignored. Third, state security prevailed over environmental health.

collective living conditions, within planetary boundaries, needs to be at the centre of governance processes and practices. In this context, we seek to address the question of how to create capabilities by exploring the two different entry points of technology and ILKS.[23]

This section substantiates our main argument by starting with some critical reflections on the capabilities approach in relation to ocean governance. It then contextualizes the conceptual foundations of global governance, arguing that the framework was developed from a top-down rather than bottom-up perspective. As a result, global governance does not leave a lot of conceptual space for the capabilities approach and ILKS to study the complex dynamics of socio-ecological systems responding to the uncertainties and rapid changes as predicted by the scientific community (IPBES, 2019; IPCC, 2023). At the same time, the contemporary ocean governance science–policy interface – as elaborated in the following section – very much excludes ILKS from governance practices and processes (see Jaeckel et al., 2023 for the case of deep-sea mining). The section continues with a discussion of how to develop capabilities for ocean governance. It concludes with some thoughts about challenges and opportunities, as looked at from the SCF.

5.1 Why Capabilities Matter to Ocean Governance

Social inequality, and with it poverty, correspond to a lack of capabilities (Alkire, 2002; Binder, 2016; Day et al., 2016; Nussbaum, 2004; Sen, 1988, 2005; Stewart, 2005; Tonon, 2018). In this context, the capability approach is essentially an overarching normative framework for the design of policies and social arrangements, and for social change in society (Robeyns, 2005), identifying the ends and means of economic development (Day et al., 2016). Among the capabilities that are necessary for more effective and equitable ocean governance, ocean protection seems to be the most relevant. Others are human adaptation and preparedness, equitable access to and sharing of information, sustainable use of resources, and the development of sustainable solutions and innovations.

Consequently, the SCF – embracing technology and ILKS as entry points – has to take into account that different communities have different needs, since they are not all equally affected by socio-ecological system change. Also, they face different risks related to the unsustainable use of ocean resources. Certainly, the relationship amongst technology and ILKS producers has never been easy. Historically, since the fifteenth century, state authorities and private

---

[23] In this context, this section will use ILKS as a broad canvass to encompass all the diversity of knowledge production and use, recognizing that this is a fairly large simplification.

companies have used technology to project power and further explore marine mineral and biological resources. As a result, IPLC have become more and more threatened by predatory economic initiatives, engendering the blue risks discussed below.

On the one hand, technoscience and technological progress has enabled faster and cheaper access to marine resources, leading to what has been called the 'blue acceleration' scenario (Blasiak, 2020; Jouffray et al., 2019). Technological solutions can also contribute to producing better public goods, for example in the management of marine life, fish stocks, and coral reefs (Sarkar et al., 2021).[24] However, technology is relatively expensive for local communities, and the diffusion is slow. Usually the 'best available technology' only exists as an aspiration in multilateral treaties. Either the available marine technology is not the best or it is only available for those who can afford it. Consequently, the 'blue acceleration' paradigm tends to reproduce the patterns of *first arrived, first served* global economic growth, coupled with social exclusion and environmental damage. Therefore, it may be a key driver for the exclusion of developing countries in the Global South. In sum, the 'blue growth paradigm' (Bennett et al., 2021) may lead to more social inequality and injustices, as discussed below.

On the other hand, the role of IPLC 'in addressing and responding to climate change and highlighting the urgent need for multilevel and cooperative action' was recognized at the Glasgow Climate Pact (Decision -/CP.26).[25] In this vein, local communities (islanders, anglers, hunters, seafood catchers, and so on), as well as Indigenous peoples, are partially isolated from scientific and technological progress, but they are holders of other types of knowledge and sustainable practices. One pertinent case is the El Niño phenomenon. It was identified by South American fishermen a number of years ago when they noticed a huge change in their catches, and then it was subsequently analysed by the scientific community, establishing the connection between El Niño patterns and climate change.

In sum, capabilities matter because the ocean has a direct influence on climate change dynamics as the regulator of global temperature and the biggest carbon sink. Solutions to ocean conservation and more sustainable use of marine resources can be very innovative and high-tech, but also nature-based, notably concerning carbon sequestration (Cohen-Shacham et al., 2016; Seddon, 2022; Seddon et al., 2021). Different actions include sustainable and climate-smart

---

[24] United Nations World Ocean Day 2023. https://unworldoceansday.org/.

[25] 26 Conference of the Parties (CoP 26, 2021). The advance unedited version, page 1. https://unfccc.int/sites/default/files/resource/cop26_auv_2f_cover_decision.pdf.

fisheries and aquaculture, restoration of ecosystems, development of renewable energy, and shipping (Lecerf et al., 2021: 4).

5.2 Conceptual Foundations

Current scholarship on global governance helps to analyse Planet Earth as a complex adaptive system. It also shows that we still must learn how to navigate the Earth system in a more sustainable way. Not only have risks related to climate change augmented, but also damages to socio-environmental systems have spread worldwide (Dalby, 2020; Haas and Western, 2020; Rockström et al., 2023). In fact, the Earth system has evolved continuously and has responded to changes that require all species to adapt to the scenarios as presented by the IPCC (AR6).[26] Realizing this challenge, the scientific community has identified boundaries to protect a 'safe operating space' for Planet Earth (Foley, 2010; Rockström et al., 2009a). Yet, the interconnectedness of those boundaries is still under-recognized (Rockström et al., 2023).

The conceptual framework of global governance evolved significantly over the years (Zelli and Möller, 2020). In the 1990s, it was mostly seen as a theoretical effort to respond to the end of the Cold War as well as the associated risks of a nuclear attack or a third world war. The consolidation of the Western liberal order under UN auspices led to more pressure on ocean resources, under the paradigm of 'freedom of the seas'. In this context, global governance was presented as the 'new superstructure' within which international organizations and the rule of law would prevail over the use of force. Multilateralism would naturally grow inside and outside the UN system to address collective action problems. There was also a plethora of perspectives on the intensification of networks taking advantage of information and communication technologies. Therefore, old challenges needed to be addressed by an increasing number of different and more diverse stakeholders in world affairs, which was thoroughly debated at the 1992 Rio Summit. Broad participation was adopted as the underlying principle of collective action to strengthen the legitimacy of environmental agendas around the world.

The turn of the century saw the adoption of new global commitments such as the UN Millennium Development Goals (2000) and the subsequent UN Sustainable Development Goals (2015). There was also a recognition of the failure of global governance mechanisms to be inclusive and to address global risks, such as climate change and human-made disasters (Guterres, 2019; Rockström et al., 2023; WEF, 2017, 2021, 2023). Concerning the ocean, UN Reports – notably IMO (2019), GEO (2019), and SOFIA (FAO, 2022) – have

---

[26] International Panel for Climate Change Sixth Assessment Report. www.ipcc.ch/report/ar6/wg1/.

shown year after year the failure to address challenges related to climate change, overfishing, aquaculture, dredging, tourism, and others. Human activities 'affecting the ocean are highly linked and interacting' (Levin and Poe, 2017: xxiii). They engender consequences such as overconsumption, pollution and contamination, ocean acidification, marine debris, invasive species, biodiversity loss, habitat degradation, and so on.

In this context of accelerated environmental degradation, Bennett and Satterfield (2018) proposed an analytical framework for environmental governance that is divided into three main elements, namely:

- institutions (laws, policies, rules, and norms);
- structures (decision-making bodies, formal organizations, and informal networks); and,
- processes (decision-making, policy creation, negotiation of values, and conflict resolution).

Their framework is useful to highlight the limited space that is left for IPLC within the global governance framework as well as the persistent challenges related to UN members' commitment to and compliance with international law. In this context, are there ways to empower IPLC? How will IPLC have access to technological innovations?

Since the diversity of stakeholders and their respective knowledge systems are of fundamental importance to Earth system governance in general (Inoue, 2018) and ocean governance in particular, they should be part of the rule-making processes in national and multilateral forums. In addition, if the negotiators do not consider the costs of ocean policies in the short, medium, and long term for all stakeholders involved, ocean governance cannot be effective. Furthermore, fighting illegal activities is part and parcel of this equation since the victims are generally the most disenfranchized communities. For example, addressing illegal, unreported, and unregulated fishing requires the collaboration of authorities, companies, Indigenous peoples, local communities, and academia, as it was in the case of Japan fighting illegal vessels near the coast of North Korea. Because the dark vessels did not inform their GPS location, it was impossible to locate them with technology alone. The collaboration of fishermen in Japan and South Korea was relevant to find the maritime outlaws.[27]

Moreover, global governance arrangements should, ideally, be informed by the capabilities of the communities affected. In other words, to deliver better public goods, ocean governance processes and practices should give voice to

---

[27] Audacious Project. Global Fishing Watch, 023. Safeguarding the Ocean by Making Human Activity at Sea Visible. Tony Long, 2023. www.audaciousproject.org.

coastal communities who are the most dependent on marine resources and vulnerable groups. But representation and delegation mechanisms do not function properly when it comes to IPLC in the national and multilateral arenas. In ocean governance, the 'power disconnect' described by Webster et al. (2020) corresponds to the distance between IPLC and policy creation processes. Although there are a few cases in which local communities participate in political processes, they are not necessarily effective in preventing the degradation of their environment, such as in the Arctic (Cone, 2006).

More specifically in the Global South, there is a significant disparity in the approaches of neighbouring countries. African and Arab countries are too different to be analysed in depth here, although the African Group is a key ocean player in the UN. Yet, Costa Rica and Bolivia are more likely to include traditional knowledge in their institutions' design efforts and laws than Brazil and Argentina, for example.[28] Other countries are exceptional, like China and India, in the sense that they are both millennium-old civilizations with *sui generis* political regimes, mixing religious faith with philosophy and medical care, and they are technological ocean powers (Tomé, 2023). But this does not mean that ILKS are included in their institutional arrangements and that Indigenous and local communities have their rights assured.

Ocean governance has some peculiarities that need to be explored in detail. First of all, it is traditionally characterized by a long-standing tension between local and national stakeholders, and their priorities. Local preferences and global stakeholder priorities do not align. The IPLC are deeply dependent on marine and coastal resources. They do not just take food from the ocean; their identity as a community is connected *to* and shaped *by* the ocean (Erinosho et al., 2022). The systemic context for maritime global stakeholders is very different by contrast, as their mode of operation is driven by economies of scale, wealth maximization, and the search for precious resources. In the Arctic and Antarctic glacial oceans, this led to several sovereign rights claims by leading countries over those territories (Scott, 2017). As a result of the critical importance of maritime trade for geopolitics and running empires, countries such as Portugal, Spain, Britain, and France heavily invested in military and diplomatic efforts over the centuries to secure maritime routes (Jones, 2021). As a result, historically, most of the international law of the seas reflected by and large the interests of Western powers, with developing countries and IPLC excluded. They are often considered as part of the so-called Global South. A better understanding of the processes of colonialism that are underlying ocean

---

[28] See for example Diva Amon's projects off the coast of Costa Rica with local researchers. In Bolivia, the Pacha Mama approach is central to this debate. See Aubertin (2021).

governance frameworks needs to inform any strategic capabilities debate because blue growth may in fact perpetuate historical social injustices (Polejack, 2022). Bennett et al. (2021: 1) synthetized them in ten points, as 'blue risks':

- dispossession, displacement, and ocean grabbing;
- environmental justice concerns from pollution and waste;
- environmental degradation and reduction of ecosystem services;
- livelihood impacts for small-scale fisheries;
- lost access to marine resources needed for food security and well-being;
- inequitable distribution of economic benefits;
- social and cultural impacts;
- marginalization of women;
- human and Indigenous rights abuses; and,
- exclusion from governance.

Second, IPLC produce knowledge that seldom escapes the local level, primarily because their capabilities are dispersed, and their knowledge is transmitted through oral history and storytelling but also because public authorities often do not give them the opportunity to speak (ex-ante focus in the decision-making process). Ranging from fishing capabilities to observing the ocean, their capabilities are also part of their collective memories and expectations for the future.

Third, IPLC, by comparison, create little environmental impact on the islands and in the coastal areas because they know they depend on the environmental health and ecosystem vitality of their settlements (St. Martin and Olson, 2017).[29] However, they are the victims of large-scale land-based and maritime impacts. Plastics and microplastics, as well as fossil fuels from ships, for example, are telling examples of unsustainable practices from companies and consumers that directly threaten their livelihoods (Cone, 2006; Onink et al., 2021). For this reason, the polluter-pays principle was included in the 2023 BBNJ Treaty, and its future translation into marine policies may generate capabilities to provide some remedies. Nonetheless, the legal principle of 'common but differentiated responsibilities' (CBDR), as it was formalized at the Rio Earth Summit in 1992, has not yet been applied to the ocean. According to the Guterres Report (2019: 52), developed countries have a material footprint that is more than thirteen times higher than that of less developed countries. This consumption pattern can be translated into ocean governance in the following way. Countries with large-scale fisheries are not necessarily those with the highest human development indexes (HDI), but they also export a lot. China

---

[29] Retrieved from Environmental Performance Index. https://epi.yale.edu/. Accessed 2 June 2023.

ranks first and accounts for around 32 per cent of the total, including fish captures and fast-increasing aquaculture. Japan, India, the United States, the Russian Federation, and Indonesia follow.[30] Yet, limiting the question to the quantity of marine protein intake only provides a partial picture, because it does not look at the capabilities of local communities and potential alternative options. According to the FAO, '[i]n low-income food-deficit countries (LIFDCs), fish consumption increased from 4.0 kg in 1961 to 9.3 kg in 2017, at a stable annual rate of about 1.5 percent'.[31] In sum, the 'historical responsibility' of those Tomé (2023: 65) has defined as marine technological powers is not adequately considered within the ocean governance frameworks, which poses significant challenges not only for justice and fairness but also institutional, agenda-setting, and capabilities considerations.[32] The critical question is whether we can envisage a more equitable, responsive, and effective 'transformative governance' (Chan, 2019; Cisneros-Montemayor et al., 2021; Erinosho et al., 2022) without tackling the historical responsibilities of marine technological powers vis-à-vis IPLC. Do we need a new legal principle that requires technology holders to protect ILKS in ocean governance?

Finally, in 2023, two key legally binding international instruments enriched ocean governance: the mining code under the auspices of the International Seabed Authority, and the BBNJ. Both instruments are based on the United Nations Convention on the Law of the Seas. Although they may bring direct impacts for the climate change agenda in terms of energy production and carbon dioxide storage, this nexus was hardly considered (Levin et al., 2020; Queiroz et al., 2023; Rockström et al., 2023). The mining code will regulate the permission for mining activities in areas beyond national jurisdiction (Ardron et al., 2023). For the time being, member countries did not agree on the rules for deep seabed mining activities (Campanella, 2024).[33] The BBNJ is based on five pillars: marine genetic resources, including questions on the sharing of benefits; area-based management tools, including marine protected areas; environmental impact assessments; capacity building and the transfer of marine technology; and cross-cutting issues.[34] While it is very difficult to assess the extent of the

---

[30] www.fao.org/3/X8002E/x8002e04.htm#:~:text=The%20global%20patterns%20of%20fish,the %20Russian%20Federation%20and%20Indonesia.

[31] www.fao.org/3/ca9229en/online/ca9229en.html#chapter-1_1. Accessed 2 January 2022.

[32] The group varies according to activities, but the core group of marine powers is composed of the United States, the European Union, China (superpowers) and then Germany, Russia, India, Indonesia, and Japan.

[33] During the July 2023 talks at ISA, based on the demand for a moratorium from the scientific community, the number of countries supporting the ban, the moratorium, or the ten-year precautionary pause on commercial mining increased to twenty.

[34] www.iucn.org/theme/environmental-law/our-work/oceans-and-coasts/marine-biodiversity-areas-beyond-national-jurisdiction-bbnj. Accessed 2 January 2022.

participation of IPLC in the domestic and multilateral decision-making process, available reports and literature seldom mention them properly. Moreover, the participation of small island states in the BBNJ negotiation processes was marked by three groups (CARICOM, SIDS, and SPIDS) (Tomé, 2023: 142).

In sum, ocean governance is a field in which a systems approach is essential. We could highlight that the deep ocean is the less-known part of the Planet. Therefore, the drivers of global environmental change demand a knowledge-based approach to Earth system governance. Communities can contribute to understanding natural processes that are sometimes invisible to scientists. A capabilities-focused framework therefore provides explanatory and policy leverage to navigate the system. Building pathways to transformative and inclusive governance within a context of many unknowns and deep uncertainties is the main challenge for ocean governance.

As Levin and Poe (2017) stressed, if we want to address quality of life on Earth, the implications of environmental change for humanity must be understood. What connects ILKS and technology is the fundamental agreement that knowledge is the sine qua non in better understanding the Earth system. What Indigenous peoples and local communities have been teaching us concerns relationships, not the accumulation of wealth (Pereira et al., 2023). In this sense, Earth is our mother, and the ocean is our father. Without a healthy ocean, we cannot improve quality of life on Earth. As humans, we are part and parcel of ocean governance, not the owner of the ocean, according to different IPLC ontologies and epistemologies. Their lesson is clear: we must not destroy our sources of livelihood and saw off the branch we are sitting on. In other words, we have the responsibility to protect life.

In this context, science has a key role to play, as will be discussed in the next section.

5.3 Navigating the Science–Policy Interface

Charting the science–policy interface implies identifying knowledge gaps and risks. Geography books usually show five oceans. But in fact there is only one ocean, since the Arctic and the Antarctica basin form a single system that connects the whole of the marine water body. As a result, the ocean is connected to Earth and the atmosphere, a fact that is often underappreciated. Knowledge and information about the ocean is not properly shared around the world, that is people do not necessarily have access to the best available scientific knowledge, and ILKS are not necessarily considered by scientists and authorities. In other words, there is still a stark divide between scientific knowledge and ILKS. As an example, technological innovation projects for ocean-climate interventions with giant companies rarely include IPLC. Some pertinent examples are CO_2 storage and air capture, cloud seeding, iron fertilization, alkalinity addition, and artificial upwelling, among others (GESAMP, 2019).

Although scientific knowledge is often mentioned in multilateral negotiations to build global governance, it is hardly accessible for Indigenous and local communities. For example, the CoP 26 Glasgow Climate Pact (2021) acknowledged the importance of Indigenous peoples and local communities as key stakeholders, but this does not mean that IPLC share a global identity and have a common understanding about how they could form 'transnational advocacy networks', as conceptualized by Keck and Sikkink (1998).

To tackle the challenge of 'ocean literacy', the United Nations Decade of Ocean Science (2021–2030) has promoted a shared information system, departing from the motto 'The science we need for the ocean we want'.[35] Authorities and scientists agreed that 'capacity development' and 'ocean science' are necessary to shape the future. The 'Ocean Decade' is connected to the UN 2030 Agenda for Sustainable Development in general and to Sustainable Development Goal 14 'Life below water' in particular. As Peter Thomson, the UN Special Envoy for the Ocean, declared: 'Ocean science, supported by capacity development, is essential not only to inform SDG 14 but also other SDGs that have an ocean dimension'. Furthermore, Dr Sue Barrell, former Chief Scientist at Australia's Bureau of Meteorology, added:

> The oceans are critical drivers of global climate and weather-related natural hazards. Deeper insights on ocean science, powered by enhanced ocean observing and data sharing systems, will dramatically advance understanding and modelling of the whole earth system and benefit all people, everywhere.[36]

Nonetheless, IPLC representatives are still disenfranchised. From a complex system and Strategic Diplomacy perspective, technology and traditions correspond to different entry points to navigate the Earth system and think of desirable futures.[37] While traditional knowledge is produced by Indigenous and local communities to address key issues related to the oceans, the best available knowledge is produced by the scientific community, the army, and big companies (technology leaders).

---

[35] www.oceandecade.org/.   [36] www.oceandecade.org/.

[37] Despite the fact that we think of the planet as one, it has no legal status so far. Likewise, humankind and governance are not clearly defined in law. In addition, the planet is divided in part under national jurisdiction and the rest (*res communis* or *res nullius*). Consequently, international public law and international environmental law need to evolve to respond to the challenges of the Anthropocene.

Tapping into the traditional wisdom of different communities is key for coping with the rapid changes of Earth system transformations. But their sustainable way of life was not generally recognized in the recent past. For people who are economically development-prone, traditional communities were the main obstacles to 'human progress' such as building roads, ports, and railways. Because they did not struggle to amass resources and transform nature for their own benefit, they were seen as underdeveloped communities that should be integrated in the 'civilized world'. Consequently, traditional communities took centuries to achieve some political space to advocate for their right to choose their future paths. While Indigenous and local communities have proved their capabilities of sustainably using ocean resources, they demand recognition of their interests and rights in decision-making processes in local, national, and multilateral arenas.

Technology producers and users, on the contrary, with high-tech mining and fishing equipment, satellites, and bioprospecting methods represent at the same time the biggest risks to resource depletion and pollution, as well as the solutions. In addition, climate change risks and solutions, as discussed in Section 4, may have irreversible impacts on ocean health and ecosystem vitality (IPCC, 2023). Providing mutual recognition and better connections for those two groups of knowledge producers is still a key challenge.

5.4 Developing Capabilities for Ocean Governance

While climate and ocean governance are deeply connected, their institutional responses were very different in the last four decades. However, there are also common points, such as the coexistence of technology/scientific and traditional knowledge production. Scientific knowledge prevails over traditional knowledge in both cases, notably after the creation of the IPCC and other scientific bodies alike (IPBES, Intergovernmental Oceanographic Commission (IOC/UNESCO), UN GEO, and the future IPOS).[38] Moreover, scientific knowledge still has plenty of huge gaps related to unexplored parts of the ocean and the effects of climate change (and engineering projects shown in Section 4).

Another point in common was the political alliance of Small Island Developing States for multilateral talks, or like-minded groups, when they decided to unite to form a majority in multilateral talks and have a voice to advance their own capabilities and priorities (Tomé, 2023). Although they vary in terms of agenda and composition, they could share a common basis of

---

[38] The International Panel on Ocean Sustainability will be officially launched in 2025, during the United Nations Ocean Conference. www.cnrs.fr/en/track-creation-ipos-new-international-panel-ocean-sustainability. Accessed 14 July 2023.

knowledge and interests. One example is the demand from the Global South to the most developed countries for marine technology transfer, capacity building, funding, and information sharing, including digital sequencing information. All of them were included in the 2023 BBNJ Treaty. This constitutes a potential entry point for co-production of policies based on the capabilities approach.

In terms of governance institutions, practices, and processes, the ocean regime is much older than the climate one, but the latter evolved much faster, being belatedly and only partially connected to the ocean. Consequently, climate geoengineering does not always take impacts on ocean health into account. Can IPLC help to build the bridge between these two international regimes? They can certainly contribute with climate-smart approaches to fisheries and aquaculture, for example.

Concerning responses, the climate regime is as complex as the ocean regime when it comes to the use of new technologies. As a matter of fact, the 'big solutions' to the challenges depend more on a few 'technological powers', and big companies, than on the other 190 countries, as shown in Section 4. In other words, there is a growing concentration of power in the hands of a few decision-makers that will most likely continue to threaten Indigenous and local communities' ways of life if there is no effective transformative change. Three cases worthy of future research are: (i) the negative effects of wind farms along the coast of countries like Brazil; (ii) the Arctic Ocean trade and geopolitical infrastructure, which pollute and contaminate what polar communities call 'the mother snow'; and (iii) the expected 2023 'super' El Niño.

For the technology entry points, the positive points are as follows: in the case of exploitation of living resources, technologies enable cheaper activities since further and deeper resources become more economically viable. In the case of bioprospecting and farming, it is a driver to improve food and health security. It increases the options for adaptation and resilience strategies. It can provide fast and effective technical solutions in contrast to endless diplomatic talks. It enables data production and modelling to monitor planetary boundaries. For the ILKS entry points, the ocean is perceived as a 'hero' who protects communities, not the victim of humankind. Risk-limiting traditional routines help ensure a more sustainable use of resources for future generations. The scope and scale of the use of resources are less predatory than industrial initiatives.

However, negative points are also relevant. For the technology entry point, uncertainties related to unintended consequences and risk management are key. Also, social justice and environmental conservation are not necessarily considered on a planetary scale. Therefore, it may lead to more power disconnection, because IPLC are usually excluded from the decision-making processes. Innovation and inventions depend heavily on a few actors, like technological powers and big companies. For the ILKS, they are related to local experiences, generally not well described and adopted by the scientific community. Also, traditions are being lost because fishermen and other communities cannot afford to keep their routines and income. Finally, traditional knowledge is sometimes based on beliefs and not easily transferred to the scale and scope of global governance (replicability).

To a large extent, the weak points of technology used for ocean governance are comparable to climate governance. The new technologies may aggravate the risks mentioned under the paradigm of 'blue growth'. The intensive use of technology for exploitation activities may lead to more food insecurity and biodiversity loss for developing countries and islands. They may also cause unintended consequences, irreparable damages, and compromise risk management. In all cases, traditional communities are unable to confront predatory large-scale activities, be they state-led or private.

In sum, an entry point for the capabilities approach is to connect technology and ILKS in the domestic political arenas, so that multilateral talks become effectively more inclusive and legitimate.

5.5 Challenges and Opportunities for Ocean Governance

Using a capabilities-centred approach to add value to the debate on strategic capabilities, this section started with a succinct contextualization of the concept of global governance, before discussing ocean governance. Then it showed the policy–science interface and used the capabilities approach to highlight three main findings.

The first finding is that ocean governance was promoted under the UN auspices, as a top-down process based on geopolitics and international law. Indigenous people, local communities, and islands in the Global South were usually underrepresented, underfunded, and deprived of effective participation. For the high seas regime since the sixteenth century, they hardly had a voice and ILKS are rarely employed. In both cases, there is a 'power disconnect' which needs to be tackled, because the more relevant to geopolitics, the less IPLC can participate in policy creation. However, concerning the islanders, they managed to participate collectively in the 2023 BBNJ talks in New York, although they fought for their survival, given their high vulnerabilities. Nonetheless, the same cannot be stated in relation to the ISA mining code negotiation process, in which a few islanders promoted deep-sea mining as if they were not the most vulnerable people. If islanders had access to scientific knowledge, they would most likely not support mining in areas beyond national jurisdiction, because we can only protect what we understand. The entry point here concerns broad inclusion in multilateral decision-making processes so that communities become full stakeholders, not only victims or targets. If power is concentrated in the hands of a few decision-makers, the future of IPLC will remain compromised. Another entry point is that we need scientists from IPLC so that they can better connect with their people. For example, those trying to save dying reefs with coral gardening or the sustainable use of mangrove resources and seafood.

Secondly, while small-scale problems have the potential to become tipping points with large-scale, system-changing consequences, those problems are usually ignored, because knowledge is still largely lacunary. So are large-scale problems, as if the ocean could heal from all human activities and aggressions, such as nuclear testing, oil spills, offshore drilling, mining, pollution, acidification, and overfishing. Moreover, problems stemming from the blue acceleration are also underestimated, even though they have been following the patterns of exclusion and degradation from land-based activities. In this regard, we contend that the blue economy (Amon et al., 2022) must not reproduce the same risks from the last century. The entry point should be similar to the polluter-pays principle so that the causes and consequences of human action stay coupled. This means that the externalities of ocean activities must be seriously estimated with impact assessment tools. Because we are all connected in the Earth system, ocean literacy must include all the knowledge and practices available, and promote the education of young people toward more sustainable practices.

Finally, technology is a powerful entry point to help solve human-made problems and to limit risks concerning climate, food, as well as environmental and health security. But there is a gap between the production and use of technology. Equally, ILKS may have the potential to tackle the same challenges, but only under the condition of its adequate recognition as a legitimate entry point for policy co-creation. Because ILKS can show others how to live in harmony with nature, they are vital for a fairer ocean governance architecture. However, Indigenous peoples and local communities also need to understand their current situation from the most recent scientific findings, such as the IPCC and IPBES reports. Likewise, decision-makers need to learn from traditional knowledge holders that the ocean supports life on Earth. It is not an open space with infinite free resources to be exploited in an unsustainable manner as if there were no tomorrow. Environmental tipping points are already part of our lives, such as marine biodiversity loss. Therefore, to improve ocean governance, we must conceptualize the 'responsibility to protect' from ILKS holders as the most important entry point to technology users.

6 Findings

As the Fourth Industrial Revolution gains pace, humanity has reached a fork in the road. Industrialization has been a history of human progress and welfare driven by the belief in functioning markets and cycles of technological innovation that have become both shorter and faster. However, industrialization has also led to the rapidly deteriorating health of the Earth system, with the human footprint triggering tipping points in the Earth's climate that, if unattended, will make natural habitats uninhabitable. Unprecedented innovation and technological transformation may, on the one hand, provide us with, to paraphrase Charles Dickens, 'the best of times' to improve planetary health. On the other hand, it may also lead to 'the worst of times' if those technologies remain untamed and simply accelerate the current unsustainable trajectory of the Earth system. In a nutshell, humanity is at the precipice that may either lead to 'the season of Light' or 'the season of Darkness', 'the spring of hope' or 'the winter of despair'.

This final section synthesizes the findings of this Element considering the SCF we developed to study and steer complex socio-ecological systems. Our primary objective as a global team of scholars from diverse academic backgrounds has been to innovate ideas to achieve Sustainable Ecological Capacity (Holland, 2008b), understood as a mega-capability that constitutes the sine qua non for the enhancement of individual and collective living conditions within planetary boundaries. In doing so, in this section, we flesh out the connection between the diverse leverage points of technology and ILKS for Sustainable Ecological Capacity. Table 2

Table 2 The strategic capabilities matrix for sustainable ecological capacity – synthesis

	Technology	**ILKS**
Strengths	• Mitigating 'the tragedy of the commons' (Hardin, 1968) • Targeting Earth system design, subset of mitigation • Navigating Earth system feedback loops and tipping points • Accelerating speed and amplifying scale of Earth system adaptation and transformation	• Community-based approach • ILKS as public good • Targeting Earth system paradigms • Sustaining livelihoods and connecting with nature • Aligning Earth system goals and designs with safe and sustainable planetary boundaries

Table 2 (cont.)

	Technology	ILKS
	▪ Addressing climate emergencies ▪ Providing damage control and palliative care ▪ Buying time	
Weaknesses	▪ Agent-based approach ▪ Technology and technological innovation as private good ▪ System goal of wealth maximization in competition with safe and sustainable planetary boundaries ▪ Potential lock-in effects, especially vis-à-vis SRM: Plan B may permanently become Plan A ▪ Exacerbating inequality and social exclusion ▪ Lack of effective governance structures ▪ Unintended consequences	▪ Highly localized domain and undervaluation limit potential impact in mitigating the root causes of climate change ▪ Lack of voice and representation in existing national, regional, and global governance frameworks ▪ Lack of academic literature on how to mobilize ILKS for addressing climate change

provides a snapshot of our findings, which will be further contextualized in this section. The critical challenges are threefold: first, taming technology for a sustainability revolution; second, amplifying voice and representation of ILKS in Earth system governance; and third, realigning the relationship between social and ecosystems, that is the way human beings relate to and engage with their natural habitat (Pereira and Gebara, 2023; Schlosberg and Carruthers, 2010; Watene, 2013, 2016; Winter, 2022).

Our empirical sections on climate and ocean governance have amply illustrated the potential and limits of the technology and ILKS entry points in each domain. Scientific and technological innovation has the capability to provide damage control and palliative care for the Earth system, mitigating 'the tragedy of the commons' (Hardin, 1968). Yet, at the same time, cutting-edge technology by and large remains a private good in the hands of only a powerful few and may increase social inequality and exclusion, if it is not accessible to everyone. In contrast, ILKS are public goods by nature but usually confined to the local level. Pursued in isolation, technology and ILKS will not meet their potential to enhance individual and collective living conditions. Yet together they may trigger systemic trans-formations, because within a socio-ecological system, local interventions can add up and generate impact at multiple scales. For that, Indigenous and local commu-nities need to have recognition, representation, and voice.

6.1 Towards an Integrated Framework of Knowledge Co-production

Building capabilities for Earth system governance therefore constitutes more than just a top-down global effort; it ought to be a polycentric (Ostrom, 2009a), a multi-scale exercise bringing diverse constituencies together in securing a climate-safe future. Designing effective institutions and integrating diverse knowledge systems for stronger socio-ecological system interventions in gen-erating Sustainable Ecological Capacity is the key challenge here.

As we have shown, pursuing Earth system governance through the technol-ogy entry point primarily impacts system design, triggering technological advance or social transformation. It also helps with navigating Earth system feedback loops and tipping points. The ILKS, on the other hand, tend to target the paradigms and goals underlying the socio-ecological system. They may also be strong candidates for social tipping points for rapid decarbonization, trigger-ing system-wide effects that are contagious and hard to stop. Across the globe, ILKS are repositories for alternative paradigms about how the world works, the connection of people with nature, and how to live sustainably within safe planetary boundaries. Yet, it would be unrealistic, if not naïve, to expect that 'the international community' would simply switch from one wealth- and profit-maximizing paradigm to another one that is more sustainable. Hence, in the Introduction to this Element we posed the question of the appropriate paradigm that will secure both survival and the continued progress of humanity. If we can agree that the paradigm of industrialization driven by profit and wealth maximization is not sustainable, what do responsible and sustainable interven-tions in our rapidly deteriorating Earth system look like? Some middle ground is needed that weaves alternative thinking and paradigms into existing Earth system governance practices and processes at the local, regional, and global levels. As Pereira and Gebara (2023: 16) observed vis-à-vis the Amazon, 'flexibility in integrating indigenous understandings into Western cognitive systems is fundamental' if we want to make some progress. Yet this also necessitates some form of recognition that Western conceptualizations of ecosystems like forests or the ocean follow restrictive utilitarian ontologies that do not embrace the spiritual or symbolic dimensions of nature transcending the material.

In this Element, we have argued for a conscious and conscientious effort to mutually reinforce the technology and ILKS entry points in creating capabilities for enhancing the individual and collective living conditions of human beings, within safe and sustainable planetary boundaries.[39] Harnessing the largely untapped potential of ILKS while reaping the benefits of technological innovation in a sustainable way calls for a polycentric approach that allows for knowledge co-production, experimentation, and learning at multiple levels of governance. This raises the question of how to connect and mutually reinforce the entry points of technology and ILKS to facilitate new collaborative forms of knowledge mobilization and creation across multiple sub-systems. Rather than privileging one entry point over another, there is strong demand for a robust and resilient integrated framework for academic and policy engagement that weaves together Indigenous knowledge and the scientific method.

Such an integrated framework needs to target the system design and the boundaries of socio-ecological systems:

1. For effective integration, the system parameters ought to be expanded, not only including but also moving IPLC into the centre of the system.
2. The institutions and social structures that shape the design of socio-ecological systems must provide voice and representation for IPLC.
3. Knowledge co-production, in essence, must be a system design intervention that becomes part and parcel of the daily grind of policy development, design, and delivery.

Weaving together Indigenous knowledge and the scientific method therefore requires an ILKS & Technology Knowledge Co-production Interface established *within* the social structures, relationships, and institutions that govern socio-ecological systems (see Figure 3). We have identified three design principles underlying the knowledge co-production framework, derived from our analysis in Section 2: *epistemological parity*; *plurality of worlds and world-views*; and *shared decision-making at the centre of policy development, design, and delivery*.

---

[39] As explained in Section 2, we do not attempt to prescribe a one-size-fits-all list of capabilities in the quest for Sustainable Ecological Capacity, as the circumstances across societies and local communities differ vastly. Yet we have offered a framework for public debate about the challenges and opportunities of the ILKS and technology entry points.

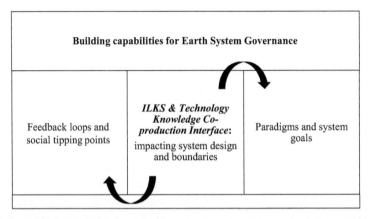

Figure 3 Knowledge co-production and learning for sustainable ecological capacity

The relationship dynamics and flows within the boundaries of such systems can trigger new dampening or amplifying feedback loops, with the capability of system change, impacting paradigms and system goals.

6.2 The Way Forward

Moving forward, how can IPLC reach their full potential considering the barriers to voice and representation in existing national, regional, and global governance frameworks? How can we mobilize Indigenous knowledge that is usually confined within a highly localized domain?

Recent government and funding initiatives may provide a clue about how to make progress. For example, the National Science Foundation of the United States launched a research programme in 2016, *Navigating the New Arctic*, probing the wide-ranging impact of climate change in the Arctic Circle, specifically encouraging scientists to collaborate with Indigenous residents in this endeavour. Similar initiatives can be found by Canada's Natural Sciences and Engineering Research Council and New Zealand's Ministry of Business, Innovation and Employment. UNESCO and the Intergovernmental Science-Policy Platform on Biodiversity and Ecosystem Services have made similar moves. Yet, while those moves reflect the right intention, there are still concerns, often expressed by Indigenous communities themselves, that those statements amount to token gestures to satisfy more inclusive funding policies rather than shifting mindsets (Sidik, 2022).

At stake is the development of shared governance structures and processes within which ILKS have epistemological parity (Kalafatis et al., 2019). A recent initiative of New Zealand's Environmental Protection Agency (EPA) is noteworthy here, because it is one of the strongest examples we have encountered so far on how to deliver on the design principles of epistemological parity, plurality of worlds and worldviews, as well as shared decision-making. The EPA initiated a new work programme to integrate Māori knowledge and perspectives into its environmental impact assessment framework. The Agency's approach to knowledge co-production is symbolized by a double-hulled canoe (*waka hourua*), representing two knowledge systems – *Mātauranga* and science – progressing in the same direction. According to the EPA (2020: 15), '[t]his visual metaphor acknowledges the contribution each knowledge system makes towards environmental management. It also symbolises that the EPA is equipping itself to embark on a voyage of discovery'.

At the heart of the impact assessment is *Mātauranga*, 'the pursuit of knowledge and comprehension of *Te Taiao* – the natural environment – following a systematic methodology based on evidence, and incorporating culture, values, and world view' (EPA, 2020: 9). Māori operate on a systems view of the world (*whakapapa*) that appreciates the interconnectedness of living and non-living things. Most importantly, as Watene (2016: 293) has observed, '[a]s kin, we have an obligation to enhance the natural world just as the natural world (as our kin) has an obligation to enhance our lives'. Impact assessment is therefore not only based on a holistic understanding that matters are embedded in a wider systemic context but also on the clear understanding of the mutual responsibilities between human beings and the natural world. In essence, this is a social compact between human beings and the natural world, with 'trustee obligations – obligations to protect, enhance and conserve' (Watene, 2016: 292). Those mutual obligations are of vital importance, as they connect past, present, and future. As Winter (2022: 37) stresses, '[i]t is conceivable, indeed likely, that climate change and environmental destruction will deny future generations their core capabilities'. Human beings and the natural world are therefore bound by an intergenerational compact with mutual rights and responsibilities.

Economic impact, in this context, would need to be considered together with impact on health and well-being as well as the environment. While this approach is different from science-technology knowledge systems, it is based on codified knowledge and techniques that are verified, tested, and updated over time (Hikuroa, 2018). Weaving *Mātauranga* and science into EPA's decision-making is about enhancing capabilities in environmental risk assessment.

Assessing impact covers four interconnected dimensions that are directly derived from *Mātauranga* (see Figure 4):

- Māori cultural concepts, customs, values, and practices that embrace ideas of environmental guardianship and stewardship;

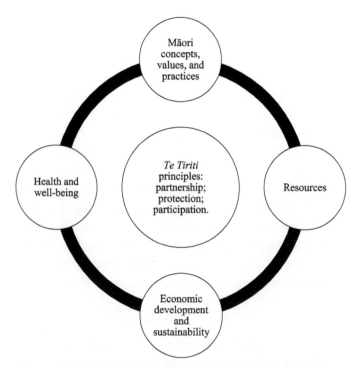

Figure 4 New Zealand EPA impact assessment (EPA, 2020)

- Resources, for example air, land, water, and ecosystems; geothermal resources; and artefacts;
- Economic development and sustainability, which includes the ability of Māori to live in an economically viable and sustainable way;
- Health and well-being – spiritual, mental, and physical – including the responsibility and capacity to operate effectively as part and parcel of a collective.

Underlying those four dimensions informing impact assessment are the set of key principles laid out in the 1840 Treaty of Waitangi (*Te Tiriti*) that historically provided for the protection of Māori culture, while the British Crown was given the right to govern and represent New Zealand: partnership; protection of Māori interests; and, participation in decision-making based on reciprocity, mutual benefit, and equal status.

In Australia, the *2019 Partnership Agreement on Closing the Gap* between federal and state governments and the Aboriginal and Torres Strait Islander communities may serve as another pertinent example of how knowledge co-production can be implemented at the policy level. According to Pat Turner (2022), the

Aboriginal lead convener of the seventy-strong coalition of Indigenous bodies representing peoples in areas including health, land, early childhood, education, business, housing, and legal services, *Closing the Gap* 'is about shared decision making with governments to ensure the full involvement of Aboriginal and Torres Strait Islander peoples at the national, state and local or regional level and embedding their ownership and expertise to close the gap'. At the same time, the agreement provides Aboriginal and Torres Strait Islander communities with full access to, and the capability to use, scientific data that is locally relevant to take more informed decisions in enhancing the individual and collective living conditions of people. Yet there is still the challenge of moving this agreement from rhetoric to reality. In March 2023, Australia appointed its inaugural Ambassador for First Nations People, leading the government's efforts in embedding First Nations' perspectives into Australia's foreign policy.[40] As an office holder of the Department of Foreign Affairs and Trade, the Ambassador will give voice and representation to First Nations People and progress their rights and interests globally.

6.3 Conclusion

In conclusion, facing the increased probability of abrupt and potentially irreversible Earth system tipping points calls for new policy pathways based on collective capabilities rather than utilitarianism. Initiatives such as *Navigating the New Arctic*, *Closing the Gap*, or New Zealand EPA's *Mātauranga* impact assessment framework highlight the need for reappraising the social contract between Indigenous and local communities, businesses, and governments. Embracing technology and ILKS in tandem can have mutually reinforcing effects. Together they can be considered *sustainability interventions* (Abson et al., 2016; Ostrom, 2009b) to tackle unsustainable human development and to enhance individual and collective living conditions within safe and sustainable planetary boundaries. In order to address the magnitude of the planetary crisis, polycentric governance and sustainability interventions are the way forward. Top-down technological solutions alone can only provide partial answers and will not be able to trigger the social tipping point dynamics necessary to stabilize and transform our fragile Earth system.

---

[40] See Department of Foreign Affairs and Trade, Ambassador for First Nations People, https://www.dfat.gov.au/international-relations/themes/indigenous-peoples/ambassador-first-nations-people.

References

Abson, D. J., Fischer, J., Leventon, J. et al. (2016). Leverage Points for Sustainability Transformation. *Ambio*, 46, 30–39.

Agrawal, A. (1995). Dismantling the Divide Between Indigenous and Scientific Knowledge. *Development and Change*, **26**(3), 413–439.

Alkire, S. (2002). *Valuing Freedoms: Sen's Capability Approach and Poverty Reduction*. New York: Oxford University Press.

Alkire, S. (2005). Why the Capability Approach? *Journal of Human Development*, **6**(1), 115–135.

Alter, K. J., & Raustiala, K. (2018). The Rise of International Regime Complexity. *Annual Review of Law and Social Science*, **14**, 329–348.

Amon, D. J., Metaxas, A., Stentiford, G. et al. (2022). Blue Economy for a Sustainable Future. *One Earth*, **5**(9), 960–963.

Ardron, J., Lily, H., & Jaeckel, A. (2023). Public Participation in the Governance of Deep-Seabed Mining in the Area. In R. Rayfuse, A. Jaeckel & N. Klein, eds., *Research Handbook on International Marine Environmental Law*. Cheltenham: Edward Elgar, pp. 361–384.

Athayde, S., Stepp, J. R., & Ballester, W. C. (2016). Engaging Indigenous and Academic Knowledge on Bees in the Amazon: Implications for Environmental Management and Transdisciplinary Research. *Journal of Ethnobiology and Ethnomedicine*, **12**, 26.

Aubertin, C. (2021). Pacha Mama contre Big Brother. *Pour la Science*, **531**, 20.

Bach, L. T., Gill, S. J., Rickaby, R. E. M. et al. (2019). CO_2 Removal with Enhanced Weathering and Ocean Alkalinity Enhancement: Potential Risks and Co-benefits for Marine Pelagic Ecosystems. *Frontiers in Climate*, **11**, 7.

Belfer, E., Ford, J. D., Maillet, M. et al. (2019). Pursuing an Indigenous Platform: Exploring Opportunities and Constraints for Indigenous Participation in the UNFCCC. *Global Environmental Politics*, **19**(1), 12–33.

Bennett, N., Blythe, J., & White, C. (2021). Blue Growth and Blue Justice: Ten Risks and Solutions for the Ocean Economy. *Marine Policy*, **125**, 104387.

Bennett, N., & Satterfield, T. (2018). Environmental Governance: A Practical Framework to Guide Design, Evaluation, and Analysis. *Conservation Letters*, **1**(6), 1–13.

Berger, P. L., & Luckmann, T. (1966). *The Social Construction of Reality: A Treatise in the Sociology of Knowledge*. London: Penguin Books.

Berkes, F. (2018). *Sacred Ecology*, 4th ed., New York: Routledge.

Bernal, B., Murray, L. T., & Pearson, T. R. H. (2018). Global Carbon Dioxide Removal Rates from Forest Landscape Restoration Activities. *Carbon Balance Manage*, **13**, 22.

Biermann, F. (2018). Global Governance in the 'Anthropocene'. In C. Brown & R. Eckersley, eds., *Oxford Handbook of International Political Theory*. Oxford: Oxford University Press, pp. 467–480.

Biermann, F. (2021). The Future of 'Environmental' Policy in the Anthropocene: Time for a Paradigm Shift. *Environmental Politics*, **30**(1–2): 61–80.

Biermann, F., Betsill, M., Gupta, J. et al. (2009b). Earth System Governance: People, Places and the Planet. Science and Implementation Plan of the Earth System Governance Project. *ESG Report 1*. Bonn, IHDP: The Earth System Governance Project.

Biermann, F., & Möller, I. (2019). Rich Man's Solution? Climate Engineering Discourses and the Marginalization of the Global South. *International Environmental Agreements*, **19**: 151–167.

Biermann, F., Pattberg, P., van Asselt, H. et al. (2009a). The Fragmentation of Global Governance Architectures: A Framework of Analysis. *Global Environmental Politics*, **9**(4): 14–40.

Binder, C. (2016). A Capability Perspective on Indigenous Autonomy. *Oxford Development Studies*, **44**(3): 1–18.

Birney, A. (2021). How Do We Know Where There Is Potential to Intervene and Leverage Impact in a Changing System? The Practitioners Perspective. *Sustainability Science*, **16**: 749–765.

Blaney, D. L., & Tickner, A. B. (2013). Introduction: Claiming the International beyond IR. In A. B. Tickner & D. L. Blaney, eds., *Claiming the International*. London: Routledge, pp. 1–24.

Blasiak, R. (2020). Blue Acceleration: Our Dash for Ocean Resources Mirrors What We've Already Done to the Land. *The Conversation*, 25 January. https://theconversation.com/blue-acceleration-our-dash-for-ocean-resources-mirrors-what-weve-already-done-to-the-land-130264.

Bockstael, E., & Watene, K. (2016). Indigenous Peoples and the Capability Approach: Taking Stock. *Oxford Development Studies*, **44**(3): 265–270.

Boulet, R., Barros-Platiau, A. F., & Mazzega, P. (2016). 35 Years of Multilateral Environmental Agreements Ratifications: A Network Analysis. *Artificial Intelligence and Law*, **24**: 133–148.

Brack, D., & King, R. (2020). Managing Land-Based CDR: BECCS, Forests and Carbon Sequestration. *Global Policy*, **12**(S1): 45–56.

Brigg, M., Graham, M., & Weber, M. (2022). Relational Indigenous Systems: Aboriginal Australian Political Ordering and Reconfiguring IR. *Review of International Studies*, **48**(5): 891–909.

Brondizio, E. S., Settele, J., Díaz, S. et al. (2019). *Global Assessment Report on Biodiversity and Ecosystem Services*. Bonn, Germany: Intergovernmental Science-Policy Platform on Biodiversity and Ecosystem Services Secretariat.

Bueger, C., & Edmunds, T. (2017). Beyond Seablindness: A New Agenda for Maritime Security Studies. *International Affairs*, **93**(6): 1293–1311.

Burke, A., & Fishel, S. (2019). Power, World Politics, and Things-Systems in the Anthropocene. In F. Biermann & E. Lövbrand, eds., *Anthropocene Encounters: New Directions on Green Political Thinking*. New York: Cambridge University Press, pp. 87–108.

Cajete, G. (2000). *Native Science: Natural Laws of Interdependence*. Santa Fe, NM: Clear Light Publishers.

Campanella, V., ed. (2024). *Seabed Mining and the Law of the Sea*, London: Routledge.

Carr, W. (2018). 'This Is God's Stuff We're Messing With': Geoengineering as a Religious Issue. In J. Blackstock & S. Low, eds., *Geoengineering Our Climate? Ethics, Politics and Governance*. New York: Routledge, pp. 66–70.

Celermajer, D., Schlosberg, D., Wadiwel, D., & Winter, C. (2023). A Political Theory for a Multispecies, Climate-Challenged World: 2050. *Political Theory*, **51**(1): 39–53.

Cesarino, P. (organização, tradução e apresentação). (2013). *Quando a Terra deixou de falar: cantos da mitologia marubo*. São Paulo: Editora 34.

Chan, K. (2019). What Is Transformative Change, and How Do We Achieve It? Think Globally Act Locally. *IPBES Blog*. What Is Transformative Change, and How Do We Achieve It? IPBES Secretariat.

Cisneros-Montemayor, A., Moreno-Báez, M., Reygondeau, G. et al. (2021). Enabling Conditions for an Equitable and Sustainable Blue Economy. *Nature*, **591**: 396–401.

Climate Action Tracker (CAT). (2021). Glasgow's 2030 Credibility Gap: Net Zero's Lip Service to Climate Action. Wave of Net Zero Emission Goals Not Matched by Action on the Ground. Accessed 22 November 2021. https://climateactiontracker.org/documents/997/CAT_2021-11-09_Briefing_Global-Update_Glasgow2030CredibilityGap.pdf.

Climate Investment Funds (CIF). (2019). *The Contribution of Traditional Knowledge and Technology to Climate Solutions*. Washington, DC: World Bank.

Cohen-Shacham, E., Walters, G., Janzen, C. et al., eds. (2016). *Nature-Based Solutions to Address Global Societal Challenges*. Gland, Switzerland: IUCN.

Cone, M. (2006). *Silent Snow: The Slow Poisoning of the Arctic*. New York: Grove Press.

Cornell, S., Berkhout, F., Tuinstra, W. et al. (2013). Opening Up Knowledge Systems for Better Responses to Global Environmental Change. *Environmental Science and Policy*, **28**: 60–70.

Corry, O. (2017). The International Politics of Geoengineering: The Feasibility of Plan B for Tackling Climate Change. *Security Dialogue*, **48**(4): 297–315.

Crutzen, P. J. (2002). Geology of Mankind. *Nature*, **415**: 23.

Cuffe, S. (2021). Indigenous Leaders to Push for Land Tenure Rights as Climate Solution at COP26. *Mongabay Latam*. Accessed 24 November 2021. https://news.mongabay.com/2021/10/indigenous-leaders-to-push-for-land-tenure-rights-as-climate-solution-at-cop26/.

Dalby, S. (2020). *Anthropocene Geopolitics: Globalization, Security, Sustainability*. Ottawa: University of Ottawa Press.

Dasgupta, P. (2021). *The Economics of Biodiversity: The Dasgupta Review*. London: HM Treasury.

Davis, A., Hodgdon, B., Marti, M. et al. (2021). Territorial Finance: Empowering Grassroots Climate Action. *PRISMA*. Accessed 24 November 2021. www.prisma.org.sv/wp-content/uploads/2021/10/Territorial-Finance-PRISMA-Report-2021.pdf.

Day, R., Walker, G., & Simcock, N. (2016). Conceptualising Energy Use and Energy Poverty Using a Capabilities Framework. *Energy Policy*, **93**: 255–264.

De Stefano, A., & Jacobson, M. G. (2018). Soil Carbon Sequestration in Agroforestry Systems: A Meta-Analysis. *Agroforestry Systems*, **92**: 285–299.

Dietz, T., Ostrom, E., & Stern, P. C. (2003). The Struggle to Govern the Commons. *Science*, **302**(5652): 1907–1912.

Dil, S., Ewell, C., Wherry, A. et al. (2021). Rolling Back Social and Environmental Safeguards in the Time of COVID-19. The Dangers for Indigenous Peoples and for Tropical Forests. *Middlesex University, Lowenstein International Human Rights Clinic Yale Law School and Forest Peoples Programme*. Accessed 24 November 2021. www.forestpeoples.org/en/rolling-back-safeguards/global.

Doney, S. C., Fabry, V. J., Feely, R. A. et al. (2009). Ocean Acidification: The Other CO_2 Problem. *Annual Review of Marine Science*, **1**: 169–192.

Donner, S. D. (2007). Domain of the Gods: An Editorial Essay. *Climatic Change*, **85**: 231–236.

Dooley, K., Christoff, P., & Nicholas, K. A. (2018). Co-producing Climate Policy and Negative Emissions: Trade-Offs for Sustainable Land-Use. *Global Sustainability*, **1**(e3): 1–10.

Earth System Governance Project (ESG Project). (2018). *Earth System Governance. Science and Implementation Plan of the Earth System Governance Project*, Utrecht, the Netherlands. www.earthsystemgovernance.org/wp-content/uploads/2018/11/Earth-System-Governance-Science-Plan-2018.pdf.

Environmental Protection Agency (EPA). (2020). *Partnership in Action: The EPA's Mātauranga Framework.* Wellington: Environmental Protection Authority.

Erinosho, B., Hamukuaya, H., Lajaunie, C. et al. (2022). Transformative Governance for Ocean Biodiversity. In I. J. Visseren-Hamakers & M. Kok, eds., *Transforming Biodiversity Governance.* Cambridge: Cambridge University Press, pp. 313–338.

Escobar, A. (2016). Thinking-Feeling with the Earth: Territorial Struggles and the Ontological Dimension of the Epistemologies of the South. *Revista de Antropología Iberoamericana,* **11**(1): 11–32.

ETC Group (Action Group on Erosion, Technology and Concentration). (2018). *Hands Off Mother Earth! Manifesto against Geoengineering.* Accessed 17 September 2020. www.geoengineeringmonitor.org/wp-content/uploads/2018/10/home-new-EN-feb6.pdf.

Etchart, L. (2017). The Role of Indigenous Peoples in Combating Climate Change. *Palgrave Communications,* **3**: 17085.

Fa, J. E., Watson, J. E. M., Leiper, I. et al. (2020). Importance of Indigenous Peoples' Lands for the Conservation of Intact Forest Landscapes. *Frontiers in Ecology and the Environment,* **18**(3): 135–140.

FAO. (2020). The State of World Fisheries and Aquaculture 2020. In *Brief. Sustainability in Action.* Rome. https://doi.org/10.4060/ca9229en.

FAO. (2022). The State of World Fisheries and Aquaculture 2022. Towards Blue Transformation. Rome, FAO. https://doi.org/10.4060/cc0461en.

Foley, J. (2010). Boundaries for a Healthy Planet. *Scientific American,* **302**(4): 54–57.

Folke, C., Hahn, T., Olsson, P. et al. (2005). Adaptive Governance of Social-Ecological Systems. *Annual Review of Environment and Resources,* **30**: 441–473.

Forsyth, T. (2014). Science. In C. Death, ed., *Critical Environmental Politics – Interventions.* London: Routledge.

Freedman, L. (2013). *Strategy: A History.* Oxford: Oxford University Press.

Fuss, S., Jones, C. D., Kraxner, F. et al. (2016). Research Priorities for Negative Emissions. *Environmental Research Letters,* **11**: 115007.

Gabay, M., & Alam, M. (2017). Community Forestry and Its Mitigation Potential in the Anthropocene: The Importance of Land Tenure Governance and the Threat of Privatization. *Forest Policy and Economics,* **79**: 26–35.

Garza-Vázquez, O., & Deneulin, S. (2018). The Capability Approach. In J. Drydyk & L. Keleher, eds., *Routledge Handbook of Development Ethics.* New York: Routledge, pp. 68–83.

GESAMP. (2019). High-Level Review of a Wide Range of Proposed Marine Geoengineering Techniques. (Boyd, P. W. & Vivian, C. M. G., eds.). (IMO/FAO/UNESCO-IOC/UNIDO/WMO/IAEA/UN/UN Environment/UNDP/ISA Joint Group of Experts on the Scientific Aspects of Marine Environmental Protection). Rep. Stud. GESAMP No. 98, 144 p. www.gesamp .org/publications/high-level-review-of-a-wide-range-of-proposed-marine-geoengineering-techniques.

Goh, E., & Prantl, J. (2017). Why Strategic Diplomacy Matters. *East Asia Forum Quarterly*, **9**(2): 36–39.

Goh, E., & Prantl, J. (2020). COVID-19 Is Exposing the Complexity of Connectivity. *East Asia Forum*, 8 April. www.eastasiaforum.org/2020/04/08/covid-19-is-exposing-the-complexity-of-connectivity/.

Graham, M. (1999). Some Thoughts about the Philosophical Underpinnings of Aboriginal Worldviews. *Worldviews: Environment, Culture, Religion*, **3**: 105–118.

Grasso, M. (2019). Sulfur in the Sky with Diamonds: An Inquiry into the Feasibility of Solar Engineering. *Global Policy*, **10**(2): 217–226.

Gross National Happiness Commission. (2009). *Tenth Five-Year Plan: 2008-2013. Volume 1: Main Document*, Thimphu: Royal Government of Bhutan.

Guterres, A. (2019). *Report of the Secretary-General on SDG Progress.* https://sustainabledevelopment.un.org/content/documents/24978Report_of_the_SG_on_SDG_Progress_2019.pdf.

Haas, P., & Western, J. (2020). Governing Complexity in World Politics. *Complexity Governance & Networks*, **6**(1): 55–67.

Haass, R. (2010). The Case for Messy Multilateralism. *Financial Times*, 6 January. www.ft.com/content/18d8f8b6-fa2f-11de-beed-00144feab49a.

Hamilton, C. (2013). The Ethical Foundations of Climate Engineering. In W. C. G. Burns & A. L. Strauss, eds., *Climate Change Geoengineering: Philosophical Perspectives, Legal Issues, and Governance Frameworks*. New York: Cambridge University Press, pp. 39–58.

Hardin, G. (1968). The Tragedy of the Commons. *Science*, **162**(3859): 1243–1248.

Heyward, C. (2013). Situating and Abandoning Geoengineering: A Typology of Five Responses to Dangerous Climate Change. *PS: Political Science & Politics*, **46**(1): 23–27.

Hikuroa, D. (2018). Mātauranga Māori – The ūkaipō of Knowledge in New Zealand. *Public Policy Institute*. Policy Briefing 1/2018. University of Auckland.

Holland, B. (2008a). Ecology and the Limits of Justice. *Journal of Human Development*, **9**(3): 401–425.

Holland, B. (2008b). Justice and the Environment in Nussbaum's 'Capabilities Approach': Why Sustainable Ecological Capacity Is a Meta-Capability. *Political Research Quarterly*, **61**(2): 319–332.

Holland, B. (2014). *Allocating the Earth*. Oxford: Oxford University Press.

Holland, B. (2021). Capabilities, Well-being, and Environmental Justice. In B. Coolsaet, *Environmental Justice: Key Issues*. New York: Routledge, pp. 66–77.

Horton, J. B., Reynolds, J. L., Buck, H. J. et al. (2018). Solar Geoengineering and Democracy. *Global Environmental Politics* **18**(3): 5–24.

Hulme, M. (2014). *Can Science Fix Climate Change?* Cambridge, MA: Polity Press.

Hulme, M. (2017). Calculating the Incalculable: Is SAI the Lesser of Two Evils? *Ethics & International Affairs*, **31**(4): 507–512.

Hurrell, A. (2007). One World? Many Worlds? The Place of Regions in the Study of International Society. *International Affairs*, **83**(1): 127–146.

Hurrell, A. (2018). Beyond the BRICS: Power, Pluralism, and the Future of Global Order. *Ethics and International Affairs*, **32**(1): 89–101.

Inoue, C. Y. A. (2018). Worlding the Study of Global Environmental Politics in the Anthropocene: Indigenous Voices from the Amazon. *Global Environmental Politics*, **18**: 25–42.

Inoue, C. Y. A., & Franchini, M. (2020). Socio-environmentalism. In A. B. Tickner & K. Smith, eds., *International Relations from the Global South: Worlds of Difference*. New York: Routledge, pp. 296–314.

Inoue, C. Y. A., & Moreira, P. F. (2016). Many Worlds, Many Nature(s), One Planet: Indigenous Knowledge in the Anthropocene. *Revista Brasileira de Política Internacional*, **59**(2): 1–19.

Inoue, C. Y. A., Ribeiro, T. L., & Resende, I. S. A. (2020). Worlding Global Sustainability Governance. In A. Kalfagianni, D. Fuchs, & A. Hayden, eds., *Routledge Handbook of Global Sustainability Governance*. New York: Routledge, pp. 59–71.

Intergovernmental Oceanographic Commission (IOC). (2020). *Global Ocean Science Report 2020*. IOC, UNESCO. https://en.unesco.org/gosr.

Intergovernmental Panel on Climate Change (IPCC). (2014). *Climate Change 2014: Synthesis Report. Contribution of Working Groups I, II and III to the Fifth Assessment Report of the Intergovernmental Panel on Climate Change* [Core Writing Team, R.K. Pachauri and L.A. Meyer (eds.)]. IPCC, Geneva, Switzerland.

Intergovernmental Panel on Climate Change (IPCC). (2019a). *Climate Change and Land. An IPCC Special Report on Climate Change, Desertification, Land Degradation, Sustainable Land Management, Food Security, and Greenhouse*

Gas Fluxes in Terrestrial Ecosystems. Summary for Policymakers. Accessed 23 November 2021. www.ipcc.ch/site/assets/uploads/2019/08/4.-SPM_Approved_Microsite_FINAL.pdf.

Intergovernmental Panel on Climate Change (IPCC). (2019b). *The Ocean and Cryosphere in a Changing Climate*. www.ipcc.ch/srocc/.

Intergovernmental Panel on Climate Change (IPCC). (2021). *Climate Change 2021: The Physical Science Basis. Summary for Policymakers*. Cambridge: Cambridge University Press.

Intergovernmental Panel on Climate Change (IPCC). (2022). Summary for Policymakers. In *Climate Change 2022: Impacts, Adaptation and Vulnerability. Contribution of Working Group II to the Sixth Assessment Report of the Intergovernmental Panel on Climate Change* [H.-O. Pörtner, D.C. Roberts, M. Tignor, et al., eds.]. Cambridge, UK and New York, NY: Cambridge University Press, 3–33. doi:10.1017/9781009325844.001.

Intergovernmental Panel on Climate Change (IPCC). (2023). *Sixth Assessment Report*. www.ipcc.ch/assessment-report/ar6/.

International Maritime Organization (IMO). (2019). *Joint Group of Experts on the Scientific Aspects of Marine Environmental Protection, High-Level Review of a Wide Range of Proposed Marine Geoengineering Techniques*. London: IMO.

IPBES. (2019). Summary for Policymakers of the Global Assessment Report on Biodiversity and Ecosystem Services of the Intergovernmental Science-Policy Platform on Biodiversity and Ecosystem Services. In S. Díaz, J. Settele, E. Brondízio et al., eds. IPBES Secretariat, Bonn.

Jackson, P. T. (2011). *The Conduct of Inquiry in International Relations: Philosophy of Science and Its Implications for the Study of World Politics*. New York: Routledge.

Jaeckel, A., Harden-Davies, H., Amon, D. J. et al. (2023). Deep Seabed Mining Lacks Social Legitimacy. *npj Ocean Sustaina*, **2**(1). https://doi.org/10.1038/s44183-023-00009-7.

Jasanoff, S. (2004). The Idiom of Co-Production. In S. Jasanoff, ed., *States of Knowledge: The Co-production of Science and Social Order*. New York: Routledge, pp. 1–12.

Jervis, R. (1997). *System Effects: Complexity in Political and Social Life*. Princeton: Princeton University Press.

Jones, B. (2021). *To Rule the Waves: How Control of the World's Oceans Shapes the Fate of the Superpowers*. New York: Scribner Book.

Jouffray, J., Blasiak, R., Norstrom, A. et al. (2019). The Blue Acceleration: The Trajectory of Human Expansion into the Ocean. *One Earth*, **2**(1): 43–54.

Kalafatis, S. E., Whyte, K. P., Libarkin, J. C., & Caldwell, C. (2019). Ensuring Climate Services Serve Society: Examining Tribes' Collaborations with Climate Scientists Using a Capability Approach. *Climate Change*, **157**: 115–131.

Kanie, N., Biermann, F., & Young, O. R. (2017). *Governing through Goals: Sustainable Development Goals as Governance Innovation*. Cambridge, MA: MIT Press.

Karlsson, R. (2020). Conflicting Temporalities and the Ecomodernist Vision of Rewilding. In J. Castro Pereira & A. Saramago, eds., *Non-Human Nature in World Politics: Theory and Practice*. Cham: Springer, pp. 91–109.

Keck, M., & Sikkink, K. (1998). *Activists beyond Borders*. Ithaca, New York: Cornell University Press.

Keith, D. (2013). *A Case for Climate Engineering*. Cambridge, MA: The MIT Press.

Kopenawa, D. and Bruce A. (2015). *A queda do céu: Palavras de um xamã yanomami*. São Paulo: Companhia das Letras.

Krenak, A. (2019). *Ideias para adiar o fim do mundo*. São Paulo: Companhia das Letras.

Kukathas, C. (2010). *Reconciling Modernity and Tradition in a Liberal Society*. CIS occasional papers 121. Canberra: The Centre for Independent Studies.

Lam, D. P. M., Hinz, E., Lang, D. J. et al. (2020). Indigenous and Local Knowledge in Sustainability Transformations Research: A Literature Review. *Ecology and Society* **25**(1): 3.

Lansing, J. S. (2006). *Perfect Order: Recognizing Complexity in Bali*. Princeton: Princeton University Press.

Lansing, J. S., & Cox, M. (2019). *Islands of Order: A Guide to Complexity Modelling for the Social Sciences*. Princeton: Princeton University Press.

Lawrence, M. G., & Crutzen, P. J. (2017). Was Breaking the Taboo on Research on Climate Engineering via Albedo Modification a Moral Hazard, or a Moral Imperative? *Earth's Future*, **5**(2): 136–143.

Lecerf, M., Herr, D., Thomas, T. et al. (2021). Coastal and Marine Ecosystems as Nature-Based Solutions in New or Updated Nationally Determined Contributions. *Ocean & Climate Platform*, Conservation International, IUCN, GIZ, Rare, The Nature Conservancy and WWF.

Leis, H. R. (1999). *A Modernidade Insustentável. As críticas do ambientalismo à sociedade contemporânea*. Petrópolis: Editora Vozes, Florianópolis: Editora da UFSC.

Lenton, T. M., Held, H., Kriegler, E. et al. (2008). Tipping Elements in the Earth's Climate System. *PNAS*, **105**(6): 1786–1793.

Lenton, T. M., Rockström, J., Gaffney, O. et al. (2019). Climate Tipping Points – Too Risky to Bet Against. *Nature*, **575**: 592–595.

Leventon, J., Abson, D. J., & Lang, D. J. (2021). Leverage Points for Sustainability Transformations: Nine Guiding Questions for Sustainability Science and Practice. *Sustainability Science*, **16**: 721–726.

Levin, L., Amon, D., & Ling, L. H. M. (2020). Challenges to the Sustainability of Deep-Seabed Mining. *Nature Sustainability*, **3**: 784–794.

Levin, P., & Poe, M. (2017). *Conservation for the Anthropocene Ocean*. Amsterdam: Elsevier.

Ling, L. H. M. (2014). *The Dao of World Politics: Towards a Post-Westphalian Worldist International Relations*. New York: Routledge.

Ling, L. H. M., & Pinheiro, C. M. (2020). South–South Talk. In A. Tickner & K. Smith, eds., *International Relations from the Global South*. New York: Routledge, 317–340.

Lockley, A. (2019). Security of Solar Radiation Management Geoengineering. *Frontiers of Engineering Management*, **6**: 102–116.

Lovelock, J. (2019). *Novacene: The Coming Age of Hyperintelligence*. London: Penguin.

MacMartin, D. G., Ricke, K. L., & Keith, D. W. (2018). Solar Engineering as Part of an Overall Strategy for Meeting the 1.5°C Paris Target. *Philosophical Transactions of the Royal Society*, **376**(2119): 20160454.

Martello, M. L. (2001). A Paradox of Virtue?: 'Other' Knowledges and Environment-Development Politics. *Global Environmental Politics*, **1**(3): 114–141.

Meadows, D. H. (1999). *Leverage Points: Places to Intervene in a System*. Hartland: The Sustainability Institute.

Meadows, D. H. (2008). *Thinking in Systems: A Primer*. London: Earthscan.

Miller, C. A., & Wyborn, C. (2020). Co-production in Global Sustainability: Histories and Theories. *Environmental Science and Policy*, **113**: 88–95.

Miller, J. H. (2015). *A Crude Look at the Whole: The Science of Complex Systems*. New York: Basic Books.

Minx, J. C., Lamb, W. F., Callaghan, M. W. et al. (2018). Negative Emissions – Part 1: Research Landscape and Synthesis. *Environmental Research Letters*, **13**: 063001.

Mishra, P. (2017). *Age of Anger: A History of the Present*. New York: Farrar, Straus and Giroux.

Molen, F. van der. (2018). How Knowledge Enables Governance: The Coproduction of Environmental Governance Capacity. *Environmental Science and Policy*, **87**: 18–25.

Morrow, D. R., Thompson, M. S., Anderson, A. et al. (2020). Principles for Thinking About Carbon Dioxide Removal in Just Climate Policy. *One Earth*, **3**: 150–153.

National Intelligence Council. (2021). *Global Trends 2040: A More Contested World*. Washington, DC: National Intelligence Council.

National Research Council (NRC). (2015a). *Climate Intervention: Carbon Dioxide Removal and Reliable Sequestration*. Washington, DC: The National Academies Press.

National Research Council (NRC). (2015b). *Climate Intervention: Reflecting Sunlight to Cool Earth*. Washington, DC: The National Academies Press.

Nicholson, S., & Jinnah, S., eds. (2016). *New Earth Politics: Essays from the Anthropocene*. Cambridge, MA: MIT Press.

Noon, M. L., Goldstein, A., Ledezma, J. C. et al. (2022). Mapping the Irrecoverable Carbon in Earth's Ecosystems. *Nature Sustainability*, **5**: 37–46.

Norton-Smith, K., Lynn, K., Chief, K. et al. (2016). *Climate Change and Indigenous Peoples: A Synthesis of Current Impacts and Experiences*. Portland: U.S. Department of Agriculture, Forest Service, Pacific Northwest Research Station.

Nussbaum, M. (2000). *Women and Human Development: The Capabilities Approach*. Cambridge: Cambridge University Press.

Nussbaum, M. (2004). Beyond the Social Contract: Capabilities and Global Justice. *Oxford Development Studies*, **32**(1): 3–18.

Nuttall, M. (2012). Livelihoods in Peril: Indigenous Peoples and Their Rights. *UN Chronicle* **46**(4): 21–23.

OECD. (2021). *Perspectives on Global Development 2021: From Protest to Progress?* Paris: Organisation for Economic Co-operation and Development.

Onink, V., Jongedijk, C. E., Hoffman, M. J. et al. (2021). Global Simulations of Marine Plastic Transport Show Plastic Trapping in Coastal Zones. *Environmental Research Letters*, **16**: 064053.

Onuf, N. G. (2013). *Making Sense, Making Worlds: Constructivism in Social Theory and International Relations*. New York: Routledge.

Orsini, A., Le Prestre, P., Haas, P. M. et al. (2020). Forum: Complex Systems and International Governance. *International Studies Review*, **22**(4): 1008–1038.

Ostrom, E. (2009a). *A Polycentric Approach for Coping with Climate Change*. Policy Research Working Paper 5095. Washington, DC: World Bank.

Ostrom, E. (2009b). A General Framework for Analyzing Sustainability of Social-Ecological Systems. *Science*, **325**(5939): 419–422.

Ostrom, E. (2010). Beyond Markets and States: Polycentric Governance of Complex Economic Systems. *American Economic Review*, **100**: 1–33.

Ott, K., & Neuber, F. (2020). Climate Engineering. In Hans von Storch, ed., *Oxford Research Encyclopedia of Climate Science*. Oxford: Oxford

University Press.https://oxfordre.com/climatescience/page/eicletter/letter-from-the-editor/.

Otto, I. M., Donges, J. F., Cremades, R. et al. (2020). Social Tipping Dynamics for Stabilizing Earth's Climate by 2050. *PNAS*, **117**(5): 2354–2365.

Pádua, J. A. (2002). *Um Sopro de Destruição. Pensamento político e crítica ambiental no Brasil Escravistas (1786-1888)*. Rio de Janeiro: Jorge Zahar Editor.

Parker, A., & Irvine, P. J. (2018). The Risk of Termination Shock from Solar Geoengineering. *Earth's Future*, **6**(3): 456–467.

Parson, E. A. (2017a). Opinion: Climate Policymakers and Assessments Must Get Serious About Climate Engineering. *PNAS*, **114**(35): 9227–9230.

Parson, E. A. (2017b). Starting the Dialogue on Climate Engineering Governance: A World Commission. *Fixing Climate Governance Series Policy Brief No. 8*. Accessed 9 December 2021. www.cigionline.org/publications/starting-dialogue-climate-engineering-governance-world-commission/.

Pasztor, J. (2017). The Need for Governance of Climate Geoengineering. *Ethics & International Affairs*, **31**(4): 419–430.

Pereira, L. M., Crespo, G. O., Amon, D. J. et al. (2023). The Living Infinite: Envisioning Futures for Transformed Human-Nature Relationships on the High Seas. *Marine Policy*, **153**: 105644.

Pereira, J. C., & Gebara, M. F. (2023). Where the Material and the Symbolic Intertwine: Making Sense of the Amazon in the Anthropocene. *Review of International Studies*, **49**(2): 319–338.

Pereira, J. C., & Terrenas, J. (2022). Towards a Transformative Governance of the Amazon. *Global Policy*, **13**(S3): 60–75.

Pereira, J. C., & Viola, E. (2020). Climate Multilateralism within the United Nations Framework Convention on Climate Change. In *Oxford Research Encyclopedia of Climate Science*. Oxford University Press. https://oxfordre.com/climatescience/page/eicletter/letter-from-the-editor/.

Pereira, J. C., & Viola, E. (2022). *Climate Change and Biodiversity Governance in the Amazon: At the Edge of Ecological Collapse?* New York: Routledge.

Polejack, A. (2022). Ocean Science Diplomacy: The All-Atlantic Ocean Research Alliance case. PhD thesis. World Maritime University, Sweden.

Prantl, J. (2005). Informal Groups of States and the UN Security Council. *International Organization*, **59**(3): 559–592.

Prantl, J. ed. (2013). *Effective Multilateralism: Through the Looking Glass of East Asia*, Basingstoke: Palgrave Macmillan.

Prantl, J. (2014). Taming Hegemony: Informal Institutions and the Challenge to Western Liberal Order. *The Chinese Journal of International Politics*, **7**(4): 449–482.

Prantl, J. (2021). Reuniting Strategy and Diplomacy for 21st Century Statecraft. *Contemporary Politics*, **28**(1): 1–19.

Prantl, J., & Goh, E. (2016). Strategic Diplomacy in Northeast Asia. *Global Asia*, **11**(4): 8–13.

Prantl, J., & Goh, E. (2022). Rethinking Strategy and Statecraft for the Twenty-First Century of Complexity: A Case for Strategic Diplomacy. *International Affairs*, **98**(2): 443–469.

Queiroz, F., Cunha, G., & Barros-Platiau, A. F. (2023). *Brazil in the Geopolitics of Amazonia and Antarctica*, New York: Lexington Books.

Querejazu, A. (2016). Encountering the Pluriverse: Looking for Alternatives in Other Worlds. *Revista Brasileira de Política Internacional*, **59**(2): e007.

Quijano, A. (1992). Colonialidade y Modernidad/Racionalidad. *Perú Indigena*, **13**(29): 11–20.

Rabitz, F. (2016). Going Rogue? Scenarios for Unilateral Geoengineering. *Futures*, **84**(Part A): 98–107.

Rameka, L. (2018). A Māori Perspective of Being and Belonging. *Contemporary Issues in Early Childhood*, **19**(4): 367–378.

Ramos, A. (2013). Mentes indígenas e ecúmeno antropológico. *Série Antropologia*, **455**. www.dan2.unb.br/images/pdf/serie_antropologia/Serie_455.pdf.

Reed, I. A. (2011). *Interpretation and Social Knowledge: On the Use of Theory in the Human Sciences*, Chicago and London: The University of Chicago Press.

Reyers, B., Folke, C., Moore, M. L. et al. (2018). Social-Ecological Systems Insights for Navigating the Dynamics of the Anthropocene. *Annual Review of Environment and Resources*, **43**: 267–289.

Rickels, W., Klepper, G., Dovern, J. et al. (2011). *Large-Scale Intentional Interventions into the Climate System? Assessing the Climate Engineering Debate*. Scoping report conducted on behalf of the German Federal Ministry of Education and Research. Kiel: Kiel Earth Institute.

Robeyns, I. (2005). The Capability Approach: A Theoretical Survey. *Journal of Human Development*, **6**(1): 93–117.

Rockström, J., Gupta, J., Quin, D. et al. (2023). Safe and Just Earth System Boundaries. *Nature*, **619**: 102–111.

Rockström, J., Steffen, W., Noone, K. et al. (2009a). Planetary Boundaries: Exploring the Safe Operating Space for Humanity. *Ecology and Society*, **14**(2): 32.

Rockström, J., Steffen, W., Noone, K. et al. (2009b). A Safe Operating Space for Humanity. *Nature*, **461**: 472–475.

Rudy, A. P., & White, D. (2014). Hybridity. In C. Death, ed., *Critical Environmental Politics – Interventions*. New York: Routledge, pp. 121–132.

Sarkar, M. S. I., Chowdhury, P., Jarin, J. A. et al. (2021). Machine Learning to Understand Marine Ecosystems and Harness the Blue Economy. *Academia Letters*, Article 2619. https://doi.org/10.20935/AL2619. *(1) (PDF) Machine learning to understand marine ecosystem and harness the blue economy. Available from:* www.researchgate.net/publication/353977115_Machine_learning_to_understand_marine_ecosystems_and_harness_the_blue_economy [accessed Nov 05 2023].

Sassen, S. (2006). *Territory, Authority, Rights: From Medieval to Global Assemblages*. Princeton: Princeton University Press.

Schellnhuber, H. J., & Held, H. (2002). How Fragile Is the Earth System? In J. C. Briden & T. E. Downing, eds., *Managing the Earth: The Eleventh Linacre Lectures*. Oxford: Oxford University Press, pp. 5–34.

Schlosberg, D., & Carruthers, D. (2010). Indigenous Struggles, Environmental Justice, and Community Capabilities. *Global Environmental Politics*, **10**(4): 12–35.

Schwab, K. (2018). *Shaping the Future of the Fourth Industrial Revolution: A Guide to Building a Better World*. London: Penguin.

Scott, S. (2017). Three Waves of Antarctic Imperialism. In K. Dodds, A. Hemmings & P. Roberts, eds., *Handbook of the Politics of Antarctica*. Cheltenham: Edward Elgar, pp. 37–49.

Seddon, N. (2022). Harnessing the Potential of Nature-Based Solutions for Mitigating and Adapting to Climate Change. *Science*, **376**(6600): 1410–1416.

Seddon, N., Sengupta, S., García-Espinosa, M. et al. (2019). *Nature-Based Solutions in Nationally Determined Contributions. Synthesis and Recommendations for Enhancing Climate Ambition and Action by 2020*. Glandd: IUCN and University of Oxford.

Seddon, N., Smith, A., Smith, P. et al. (2021). Getting the Message Right on Nature-Based Solutions to Climate Change. *Global Change Biology*, **27**(8): 1518–1546.

Sen, A. K. (1977). Rational Fools: A Critique of the Behavorial Foundations of Economic Theory. *Philosophy & Public Affairs*, **6**(4): 317–344.

Sen, A. K. (1985). *Commodities and Capabilities*. Amsterdam: North-Holland.

Sen, A. K. (1988). The Concept of Development. In H. Chenery & T. N. Srinivasan, eds., *The Handbook of Development Economics*, Volume I. Amsterdam: Elsevier, pp. 10–26.

Sen, A. K. (1999). *Development as Freedom*. New York: Alfred Knopf.

Sen, A. K. (2005). Human Rights and Capabilities. *Journal of Human Development*, **6**(2): 151–166.

Sen, A. K. (2009). *Idea of Justice*. Cambridge: Belknap Press of Harvard University Press.

Sen, A. K. (2013). The Ends and Means of Sustainability. *Journal of Human Development*, **14**(1): 6–20.

Seymour, F., La Vina, T., & Hite, K. (2014). Evidence Linking Community-Level Tenure and Forest Condition: An Annotated Bibliography. *Climate and Land Use Alliance*. Accessed 24 November 2021. www.climateandlandusealliance.org/wp-content/uploads/2015/08/Community_level_tenure_and_forest_condition_bibliography.pdf.

Sidik, S. M. (2022). Weaving Indigenous Knowledge into the Scientific Method. *Nature*, **601**, 285–287.

Slaughter, A. M. (2017). *The Chessboard and the Web: Strategies of Connection in a Networked World*. New Haven: Yale University Press.

Smith, L. T. (2012). *Decolonizing Methodologies: Research and Indigenous Peoples*. London: Zed Books.

St. Martin, K., & Olson, J. (2017). Creating Space for Community in Marine Conservation and Management: Mapping 'Communities-at-Sea'. In P. Levin and M. Poe, eds., *Conservation for the Anthropocene Ocean*. Amsterdam: Elsevier, pp. 123–141.

Steffen, W., Richardson, K., Rockström, J. et al. (2015). Planetary Boundaries: Guiding Human Development on a Changing Planet. *Science*, **347**(6223): 736.

Stewart, F. (2005). Groups and Capabilities. *Journal of Human Development*, **6**(2): 185–204.

Sullivan, S., & Cropsey, S. (2018). Seablindness: How Political Neglect Is Choking American Seapower and What to Do about It. *Naval War College Review*, **71**(4): 149–152.

Svoboda, T., Buck, H. J., & Suarez, P. (2019). Climate Engineering and Human Rights. *Environmental Politics*, **28**(3): 397–416.

Talberg, A., Christoff, P., Thomas, S. et al. (2018). Geoengineering Governance-By-Default: An Earth System Governance Perspective. *International Environmental Agreements*, **18**: 229–253.

Tengö, M., Brondizio E. S., Elmqvist, T. et al. (2014). Connecting Diverse Knowledge Systems for Enhanced Ecosystem Governance: The Multiple Evidence Base Approach. *Ambio*, **43**(5): 579–591.

Tengö, M., Hill, R., Malmer, P. et al. (2017). Weaving Knowledge Systems in IPBES, CBD and Beyond – Lessons Learned for Sustainability. *Current Opinion in Environmental Sustainability*, **26–27**: 17–25.

The Royal Society. (2009). *Geoengineering the Climate: Science, Governance and Uncertainty*. London.https://royalsociety.org/-/media/Royal_Society_Content/policy/publications/2009/8693.pdf.

Thiele, L. P. (2019). Geoengineering and Sustainability. *Environmental Politics*, **28**(3): 460–479.

Tickner, A. B. (2013). By Way of Conclusion. Forget IR? In A. B. Tickner & D. Blaney, eds., *Claiming the International*. New York: Routledge, pp. 214–232.

Tickner, A. B., & Blaney, D. L. (2012). Introduction: Thinking Difference. In A. B. Tickner & D. L. Blaney, eds., *Thinking International Relations Differently*. New York: Routledge, pp. 1–24.

Tomé, C. H. R. (2023). *Power, Architecture, and Agency in the Marine Biodiversity Beyond National Jurisdiction Treaty-Making: An Earth System Governance Perspective*. PhD thesis. International Relations Institute. University of Brasilia. Brazil.

Tonon, G. (2018). Introduction: Communities and Capabilities. *Journal of Human Development and Capabilities*, **19**(2): 121–125.

Townsend, J., Moola, F., & Craig, M. K. (2020). Indigenous Peoples Are Critical to the Success of Nature-Based Solutions to Climate Change. *Facets*, **5**(1): 551–556.

Tugendhat, H. (2021). Re-thinking Nature-Based Solutions: Seeking Transformative Change Through Culture and Rights. A Briefing for the Post-2020 Global Biodiversity Framework. *Forest Peoples Programme*. Accessed 25 November 2021. www.forestpeoples.org/en/briefing-paper/2021/re-thinking-nature-based-solutions.

Turner, P. (2022). A Real Partnership with First Peoples Is Key to Closing the Gap. *The Policymaker*, 9 May. https://thepolicymaker.jmi.org.au/a-real-partnership-with-first-peoples-is-key-to-closing-the-gap/.

UK Government and United Nations Climate Change. (2021a). Glasgow Leaders' Declaration on Forests and Land Use. Accessed 25 November 2021. https://ukcop26.org/glasgow-leaders-declaration-on-forests-and-land-use/.

UK Government and United Nations Climate Change. (2021b). COP26 IPLC Forest Tenure Joint Donor Statement. Accessed 25 November 2021. https://ukcop26.org/cop26-iplc-forest-tenure-joint-donor-statement/.

UN Glasgow Climate Pact. (2021). Decision -/CP.26 Glasgow Climate Pact. https://unfccc.int/documents/310475.

United Nations. (2015). *Framework Convention on Climate Change*. FCCC/CP/2015/L.9/Rev. 1, 12 December.

United Nations. (2021). Framework Convention on Climate Change. FCCC/PA/CMA/2021/L.16, 12 November.

United Nations Climate Summit. (2014). New York Declaration on Forests. Declaration and Action Agenda. Accessed 26 November 2021. https://forestdeclaration.org/wp-content/uploads/2021/08/NYDF_Declaration.pdf.

United Nations Development Programme (UNDP). (2020). *Human Development Report 2020. The Next Frontier: Human Development and the Anthropocene*. New York.

UN Environment. (2019). Global Environment Outlook – GEO-6: Healthy Planet, Healthy People. Nairobi. DOI 10.1017/9781108627146.

United Nations Environment Programme (UNEP). (2022). *Nature-Based Solutions: Opportunities and Challenges for Scaling Up.* Nairobi.

Veit, P. G. (2021). 9 Facts About Community Land and Climate Mitigation. *World Resources Institute.* Accessed 22 November 2021. https://files.wri.org/ d8/s3fs-public/2021-10/9-facts-about-community-land-and-climate-mitiga tion.pdf.

Viola, E., & Franchini, M. (2018). *Brazil and Climate Change: Beyond the Amazon.* New York: Routledge.

Viveiros de Castro, E. (2004). Exchanging Perspectives: The Transformation of Objects into Subjects in Amerindian Ontologies. *Common Knowledge*, **10**(3), 463–484.

Wapner, P. (2010). *Living Through the End of Nature: The Future of American Environmentalism.* Cambridge, MA: MIT Press.

Wapner, P. (2014). The Changing Nature of Nature: Environmental Politics in the Anthropocene. *Global Environmental Politics*, **14**(4): 36–54.

Watene, K. (2013). Nussbaum's Capability Approach and Future Generations. *Journal of Human Development and Capabilities*, **14**(1): 21–39.

Watene, K. (2016). Valuing nature: Māori Philosophy and the Capability Approach. *Oxford Development Studies*, **44**: 287–296.

Webster, D. G., Gonçalves, L., Kim, R. et al. (2020). How Power Disconnects May Affect the Outcome of the Ongoing BBNJ Negotiations? In A. F. Barros-Platiau & C. Oliveira, eds., *Conservação dos recursos vivos em áreas além da jurisdição nacional: BBNJ e Antártica.* Rio de Janeiro: Lumen Juris, pp. 155–190.

Welsby, D., Price, J., Pye, S. et al. (2021). Unextractable Fossil Fuels in a 1.5°C World. *Nature*, **597**: 230–234.

Whyte, K. P. (2013). Justice Forward: Tribes, Climate Adaptation and Responsibility. *Climate Change*, **120**: 517–530.

Whyte, K. P. (2018). Indigeneity in Geoengineering Discourses: Some Considerations. *Ethics, Policy & Environment*, **21**(3): 289–307.

Wilson, A. C. (2004). Reclaiming Our Humanity: Decolonization and the Recovery of Indigenous Knowledge. In D. A. Mihesuah & A. C. Wilson, eds., *Indigenizing the Academy. Transforming Scholarship and Empowering Communities.* Lincoln, Nebraska: University of Nebraska Press, pp. 69–87.

Winter, C. (2022). *Subjects of Intergenerational Justice: Indigenous Philosophy, the Environment and Relationships.* New York: Routledge.

World Bank. (2022). *World Development Report 2022: Finance for an Equitable Recovery.* Washington, DC: World Bank.

World Economic Forum (WEF). (2017). *Harnessing the Fourth Industrial Revolution for the Earth*. Geneva: World Economic Forum.

World Economic Forum (WEF). (2018). *Harnessing Artificial Intelligence for the Earth*. Geneva: World Economic Forum.

World Economic Forum (WEF). (2021). *A 10-Step Plan to Save Our Seas by Douglas MacCauley*. Geneva: World Economic Forum.

World Economic Forum (WEF). (2023). *Global Risks Report*. Geneva: World Economic Forum.

World Meteorological Organization (WMO). (2020). *The Global Climate in 2015–2019*. Geneva: WMO.

World Meteorological Organization (WMO). (2023). News. July 2023 confirmed as hottest month on record, 14 August 2023, https://public.wmo.int/en/media/news/july-2023-confirmed-hottest-month-record.

Young, O. R. (2017). *Governing Complex Systems: Social Capital for the Anthropocene*. Cambridge: MIT Press.

Young, O. R., Underdal, A., Kanie, N. et al. (2017). Goal Setting in the Anthropocene: The Ultimate Challenge of Planetary Stewardship. In N. Kanie, F. Biermann & O. R. Young, eds., *Governing through Goals: Sustainable Development Goals as Governance Innovation*. Cambridge: MIT Press, pp. 53–74.

Zelli, F., & Möller, I. (2020). Global Governance in Complex Times: Exploring New Concepts and Theories on Institutional Complexity. *Complexity, Governance & Networks*, **6**(1): 1–13.

Zürn, M., & Schäfer, S. (2013). The Paradox of Climate Engineering. *Global Policy*, **4**(3): 266–277.

About the Authors

Jochen Prantl is Professor of International Relations at the Strategic and Defence Studies Centre of The Australian National University, where he is also the Associate Dean International of the ANU College of Asia and the Pacific. His research focuses on global governance, international security, and strategy and statecraft. He is the co-lead of the Strategic Diplomacy programme at ANU.

Ana-Flávia Barros-Platiau is Professor at the Institute of International Relations at the University of Brasilia and at the Superior Defense College . Director of the Brasilia Research Center at Earth System Governance (Universiteit Utrecht). Her research interests include global governance, focusing on the ocean and polar regions.

Cristina Yumie Aoki Inoue is an Associate Professor at Department of Geography, Planning and Environment, Radboud University, where she co-coordinates the Radboud Centre for Sustainability Challenges. She is also a senior researcher at the Center for Global Studies/Institute of International Relations, University of Brasília, Brazil. Her current research focuses on planetary justice, transformative governance and sociobiodiversity in the Brazilian Amazon. Cristina is a member of the Scientific Steering Committee of the Earth System Governance research network.

Joana Castro Pereira is Assistant Professor of Politics and International Relations at the Faculty of Arts and Humanities of the University of Porto (FLUP) and researcher at the Institute of Sociology within the same institution. She is also Senior Research Fellow with the Earth System Governance network and member of the Planet Politics Institute. Her research focuses on exploring the political challenges presented by the Anthropocene, studying the governance of the Amazon rainforest, and examining the international and Latin American political economy of climate change.

Thais Lemos Ribeiro is a research fellow at the Earth System Governance Network. Her current research is about methodology in the study of global environmental governance, global climate governance architecture, and environmental justice, with a focus on ontological and epistemological dimensions.

Eduardo Viola is Senior Fellow at the Institute of Advanced Studies, University of São Paulo, and Professor of International Relations at the

School of International Relations, Getulio Vargas Foundation (São Paulo). He retired from the University of Brasilia in 2018 after 39 years and is now an emeritus professor. He is also Chair of the Research Committee 51st "International Political Economy" of the International Political Science Association and Faculty of the Earth System Governance Project. He has published extensively on International Politics of Climate Change, Globalization and Governance and Climate Policy/Politics in Brazil. He has 342 quotations on the Web of Science and more than 6,300 quotations at Google Scholar.

Cambridge Elements ⹌

Earth System Governance

Frank Biermann

Utrecht University

Frank Biermann is Research Professor of Global Sustainability Governance with the Copernicus Institute of Sustainable Development, Utrecht University, the Netherlands. He is the founding Chair of the Earth System Governance Project, a global transdisciplinary research network launched in 2009; and Editor-in-Chief of the new peer-reviewed journal *Earth System Governance* (Elsevier). In April 2018, he won a European Research Council Advanced Grant for a research program on the steering effects of the Sustainable Development Goals.

Aarti Gupta

Wageningen University

Aarti Gupta is Professor of Global Environmental Governance at Wageningen University, The Netherlands. She is Lead Faculty and a member of the Scientific Steering Committee of the Earth System Governance (ESG) Project and a Coordinating Lead Author of its 2018 Science and Implementation Plan. She is also principal investigator of the Dutch Research Council-funded TRANSGOV project on the Transformative Potential of Transparency in Climate Governance. She holds a PhD from Yale University in environmental studies.

Michael Mason

London School of Economics and Political Science

Michael Mason is a full professor in the Department of Geography and Environment at the London School of Economics and Political Science. At LSE he is also Director of the Middle East Centre and an Associate of the Grantham Institute on Climate Change and the Environment. Alongside his academic research on environmental politics and governance, he has advised various governments and international organisations on environmental policy issues, including the European Commission, ICRC, NATO, the UK Government (FCDO), and UNDP.

About the Series

Linked with the Earth System Governance Project, this exciting new series will provide concise but authoritative studies of the governance of complex socio-ecological systems, written by world-leading scholars. Highly interdisciplinary in scope, the series will address governance processes and institutions at all levels of decision-making, from local to global, within a planetary perspective that seeks to align current institutions and governance systems with the fundamental 21st Century challenges of global environmental change and earth system transformations.
Elements in this series will present cutting edge scientific research, while also seeking to contribute innovative transformative ideas towards better governance. A key aim of the series is to present policy-relevant research that is of interest to both academics and policy-makers working on earth system governance.
More information about the Earth System Governance project can be found at: www .earthsystemgovernance.org.

Cambridge Elements ☰

Earth System Governance

Elements in the Series